And now, Dan Day, I have questions for you. Where in God's heaven have you been? If you can interpret the Bible like this, think theologically like this, challenge us spiritually like this, analyze human nature like this, spin a phrase like this and make us laugh like this, why haven't you been churning our souls with your writing like this for years? Will you please answer with another book like this before you meet your Maker, and the Maker asks why you did not write more for the good of the church and the flowering of humanity?

—**WALTER B. SHURDEN**
Minister at Large
Mercer University

Many Christians find it difficult to ask "hard" questions when it comes to matters of faith. There is the fear that asking questions can destroy one's faith. In *If Jesus Isn't the Answer . . . He Sure Asks the Right Questions!*, Daniel Day helps to take away the fear. With candor and honesty, he praises the value of asking questions by pointing to Jesus as a master in the "great Jewish tradition of asking 'convincing questions.'" Dan then takes a look at some of those hard questions posed by Jesus and offers, in a humble, confessional style, his own thoughts and observations. Letting us peer over his shoulder as he grapples with hard questions helps us see that growth, not fear, can come from asking.

—**KAREN G. MASSEY**
Associate Dean for Masters Degree Programs
McAfee School of Theology

Questions of faith that are asked in faith lead to more faith not less. Dan Day's exploration of Jesus' questions deepens our trust in God and broadens our view of the world. This book beautifully practices the proven method of spiritual formation known as "faith seeking understanding."

—GEORGE A. MASON
Senior Pastor, Wilshire Baptist Church
Dallas, Texas

IF JESUS ISN'T THE ANSWER . . .
HE SURE ASKS THE RIGHT QUESTIONS!

Smyth & Helwys Publishing, Inc.
6316 Peake Road
Macon, Georgia 31210-3960
1-800-747-3016

Scripture quotations are taken from the NRSV.

Library of Congress Cataloging-in-Publication Data

Day, J. Daniel.
If Jesus isn't the answer, he sure asks the right questions / by J. Daniel Day.
pages cm
ISBN 978-1-57312-797-4 (pbk. : alk. paper)
1. Theology--Miscellanea. I. Title.
BR118.D39 2015
230--dc23

2015004804

IF JESUS ISN'T
THE ANSWER…
He sure asks the right questions!

J. Daniel Day

Also by J. Daniel Day

Seeking the Face of God: Evangelical Worship Reconceived

Contents

Beware the coming of the Stranger
who knows how to ask questions.

—T. S. Eliot
Choruses from the Rock

Preface

Good manners and common sense urge writers to tell readers a little about the background of the book they hold in their hands. One truth about this book is that it's been around for a decade—at least in my mind.

The title goes back to a sentence I read years ago. If memory serves me well, I think that sentence came from the playwright Archibald MacLeish and was sent to then-famous clergyman George Buttrick. Buttrick had asked MacLeish to participate in a Christian forum of some kind. After initially declining, MacLeish reconsidered and agreed, saying, "I'm still not sure Christianity has the answers, but I do think it asks the right questions."

This book may be something of a curiosity piece. Is it a questioning book, or is it an answering book? My intention has certainly been to write something that honors the questioning spirit and encourages the search for one's faith answers. But I've also written confessionally, telling you where my mind has probed and landed in my own faith search. The candor I plead for within the book made it feel dishonest to manufacture a perplexity or total cluelessness that isn't accurate in all cases. Because of this, the book may at times seem bipolar—praising questions but also offering (my present) answers.

Perhaps, therefore, this book is better understood as a theological expression of the Colbert Nation. In recent days a nine-year run of the popular TV comedy show *The Colbert Report* came to an end. Stephen Colbert took much of America by storm in 2005 in his first show when he said that the nation was seriously divided, but not between Democrats and Republicans or conservatives and liberals. The real divide, Colbert righteously deadpanned, was "between those who think with their head and those who *know* with their *hearts*." I suspect this book contains ideas that people on both sides of Colbert's division will find unpalatable. I hope it leads both to honor good questions as golden treasures and to increase the number of questions they entertain.

The fact that I've chosen to elevate questions rather than answers will, I hope, encourage you to pursue your own questions. Such answers as I have offered are given only as testimony and observation, not as ultimatums. You will have to live your own life and wrestle with your own questions and answers. My prayers attend your journey, even as I recall my own journey. In doing so, I am reawakened to gratitude for the church folks who first loved me into belief and for those who later patiently listened as I worked through the meaning of the church's faith and my own. I hope you, too, will be blessed by such a company of patient followers of the Lamb.

I want to acknowledge the help given me at various points in this project by a circle of friends: Ed Bateman, Timothy Brock, Derek Hogan, Kelly Jones Jorgenson, and Dave Stratton. I owe them although I wouldn't want anyone to hold them accountable for what I alone have written. The thoughts in the book are mine though on more than one occasion their challenges made me rethink those thoughts. In a class by herself is Mary Carol, the lady who agreed to marry me decades ago. She continues to be a source of life and happiness for me, including being a patient listener to and frequent sharer of my questions and the search for understanding. This book is as much hers as mine, for she has been a cheerleader for the project from its inception.

With deep gratitude, I dedicate this book to churches whose people were brave enough to call me "pastor" and kind enough to teach me much about this faith life. In chronological order, those churches are Walker Baptist Church of Wynnewood, Oklahoma; Leon Baptist Church of Leon, Oklahoma; Hillcrest Baptist Church of Denton, Texas; First Baptist Church of Ruston, Louisiana; First Baptist Church of McAlester, Oklahoma; First Baptist Church of Columbia, Missouri; and First Baptist Church of Raleigh, North Carolina. I am fortunate to have served such varied but gracious people.

J. Daniel Day
Christmas 2014

Chapter 1

The Significance of Good Questions

Questions shape our lives. Even when no one speaks them, they rise silently from within, leave their calling card on the heart's door, and depart, their assignment having been accomplished.

So it was for me when, at age nine, I studied the robin I had just killed with my new BB gun. As I held the dead bird in my hand, the excitement I'd felt only moments before as I watched it fall from the tree gave way to a mixture of sadness and fear. The thing was so small and now so irreversibly dead. I lowered it reverently to the ground and slumped down beside it, stunned. *What is it like to die?* I wondered. *What is death, anyway? And who am I that, without thinking, I've caused the death of such a harmless creature?* Thus was I introduced to the long, deep thoughts of boyhood. Nobody had asked me a thing, but the chisel and hammer of big questions began to shape me.

Of course, even earlier, displeased playmates had sometimes taken their own psychological shots at me with that most philosophical of questions: *"Who do you think you are?"* Bull's-eye! Their question shaped me. Later, while lost in the pimple-marked black hole of adolescence, a top-twenty love song filled the radio waves. It wailed, "What am I living for, if not for you?" At the time, I had no female "you" to be "living for," so the first part of that song's question nabbed me: What *am* I living for? Sages in every era have dealt with that one. Six years later, dressed in a rented tuxedo and with hair slicked to a glossy sheen, I stood beside a female "you" and heard a pastor ask, "Will you have this woman to be your wife . . . for better or for worse, in sickness as in health . . . and be true to her so long as you both shall live?" A heart-stopping string of questions! However, so juiced was I at the moment by testosterone and puppy love that I hardly noticed the gravity of the questions. Today, decades deep into honoring my easy "I will," I realize how much those questions have shaped me.

The same thing applies to religion.

Occasionally I hear people complain that their parents pushed religion down their throats. I'm sure my childhood had some of that, but what I remember most isn't the force-feeding of answers. It is a question that was sung into me.

Seated in church beside my mother one Sunday morning, I listened to a soloist's words. Although our church usually had an ear-pleasing choir in place for its worship services, on that Sunday the repeated refrain from a man's voice slipped past my ears and then dropped into deep, impressionable caverns:

> I am satisfied, I am satisfied. I am satisfied with Jesus.
> But the question comes to me, as I think of Calvary:
> "Is my Master satisfied with me?"[1]

I'll leave it to others to critique the quality of the poetry. I can only speak of the impact of that concluding question. Is my Master satisfied with me? My life has been my answer, for good or ill.

Questions form us. Sometimes they do it by embarrassing us, exposing what we don't know but perhaps should have known, or revealing what we don't want others to know that we do know. Other times questions shake us awake—rudely or gently. There are moments when they nibble at the edges of easy certainties and challenge shallow assumptions and hint of sturdier foundations. Now and then they invite us to go deeper and in doing so lead us higher. Sometimes they just interrogate us and leave, their only trace being a lingering uneasiness, an unresolved wonderment. But they shape us.

Always these questions are just as important as the kinds of answers we want teachers to deposit into our children's knowledge banks. Those schoolroom answers are usually a part of what philosopher Martin Heidegger called "calculating" thought. According to Heidegger, calculating thought concerns events and formulas and data; its intent is to discover and convey correct information. But he said there's also another kind of thought, "meditative" thought, which is equally important. This kind of thought concerns the search for the meaning of things, and its intent is to discern truth.

Both kinds of thought, calculating and meditative, are needed. We do, after all, want our electricity to work and our bank statements to balance. But life is about more than circuitry and spreadsheets. It's also about anger, grief, love, death, and hope, and our questions and answers about these matters are just as important for life as is knowledge of polymers and planets. Another heavyweight European philosopher, Ludwig Wittgenstein, contended that even should science master all our *how* questions, the bigger questions of meditative thought will still be there, untouched.[2] Sometimes these meditative questions arise unsought, slashing their way into our living spaces as the result of someone's chance remark. Or perhaps they slide in from a sentence in a movie or a line from a song, or perhaps by means of a shattering event—or an exhilarating one. Other times they arrive more subtly, maybe through a raised eyebrow or a comment written in the margin of a term paper by a wily teacher. Who can tell how and from where the deep questions come? If we are honest and have our wits about us, all-important questions do pound us for answers no Google search can supply. These, I believe, are the questions that matter most; they are the questions that, if unattended, stalk our busy but disappointingly shallow lives. Conversely, if wrestled with honestly, they can open us to quiet wisdom and strength, to the kind of life Jesus might have said was fed by streams of living water.

A Fistful of Answers

Ideally, every country crossroads church and Gothic cathedral, and every other church building, would be a place that specializes in meditative, truth-probing questions that help us keep life focused and honest and deep. They'd be places sought out by wise and thoughtful people, by simple people, by curious people—by that archetypal Everyman who just wants to make some sense of life. That would be the ideal.

Unfortunately, many churches are better known as places with a fistful of ready-made answers, not places ready to receive thorny questions. One semi-humorous indicator that this is the world's perception can be found on a small plaque I saw in a pastor's office. He said it was a gift to him from his mother-in-law, soon after he married into her family. The plaque announced a "Rate Schedule" with the following fees:

Answers $ 1
Answers that require thought $ 2
Correct Answers $ 4
—Dumb looks are still free—

I hope the plaque was given in jest, but the fact that it was given to a young preacher is evidence enough that at least his mother-in-law thought he was, in some manner, in the answer business.

I probably need to pause now and clearly state that I realize a church that has *no* answers is an embarrassment. The gospel announced through the ministry of Jesus of Nazareth speaks profoundly to the deep issues of life, and the church is obliged to give witness to this treasure. This I fully understand. But I also understand that the number of answers served up by the church is often more than the number of answers authorized by the gospel of Christ. And I also believe that gospel's light is often presented as a floodlight rather than the audacious candle in the wind that it is. As in dining, presentation is everything.

One can, of course, understand why the church is known to be the answer place. Christendom has a two-millennia-long collection of bold, buttoned-down creeds and confessions that, as one exuberant preacher put it, "unscrew the inscrutable" and proclaim definitive statements about matters even angels would like to understand. Even more pointedly, zealous Christians have long preached Jesus as "the" answer, though they have been vague about what the questions were. "Christ Is the Answer" was a slogan I often saw in my teen years; it was standard copy for church marquees and was printed on banners hung above the choir loft during revival services. Today's churchgoers may be more familiar with a musical variant of the same tradition, a singable gospel song titled "Jesus Is the Answer."

As much as I identify with the conviction expressed within this tradition, I am uncomfortable enough with it to write an entire book as something of a lover's quarrel. My discomfort arises in part from the end-of-discussion manner in which all this is communicated. For instance, in the "Jesus Is the Answer" song, the lyrics say people may have questions, but no invitation is issued to voice them.[3] The song simply repeats its insistence that "Jesus is the answer," whatever your issue may be. If we were playing cards, this would be like thumping the trump card on the table—game over! But this isn't a card game. This is, or at least it needs to be, a conversation, a testimony rather than a take-it-or-leave-it verdict.

As heartfelt as the conviction within this "answer" tradition is, and even as true as its statements may be, this is not a winning strategy. The delight of discovery has forgotten the necessity of humility. People have questions that need to be heard and responded to sympathetically and dialogically—not dismissively. Life and its complexities aren't solved as simplistically as "the answer" tradition implies. Indeed, there are times when Jesus is more the problem than the answer. What he said, what he asked, what he did and what he failed to do, and how his influence still resonates after all these centuries is a continuing problem for our world. This book will contend that there is a better approach than the "answer" tradition. It's the way of turning to Jesus as "the Stranger who knows how to ask questions."

The New Testament is quite careful in its presentation of Jesus. Not to be overly picky about it, but in the New Testament Jesus is never said to be "the answer"—at least not in those precise words. Rather, Jesus is presented as "the Way" (John 14:6). Upon reflection, these two characterizations offer different images and lead in correspondingly different directions.

"The way" issues an invitation; "the answer" declares that the party's over. "The way" implies a journey; "the answer" announces a destination reached. "The way" suggests a guide; "the answer" declares a winner. Yes, the shadings here are delicate, but they are part of the complex mix of subtle factors that lead to a general perception of preachers and Christians as being people with a fistful—literally, a "fist" full—of answers rather a heart full of interest in and eagerness to hear and talk about the substantive dilemmas and questions of existence.

When Jesus is presented as *the* omnibus "answer," the skeptical have reason to be amused, wondering just how Jesus answers the questions, say, of quantum physics or genome research. Henri Nouwen captured the counterproductive nature of this reductionist tactic when he told of the Catholic parochial school teacher who asked her class, "Who invented the steam engine?" There was no reply, so the teacher repeated the question. Once again silence prevailed. Finally, after a third "Doesn't anyone know who invented the steam engine?" a little voice drearily offered, "I guess it must be Jesus again."

Most of all, "the answer" tradition sets new believers up for disillusionment when they later discover that the Christian way is a little more complicated than just "Jesus." The church that speaks only in "the answer" voice can rightly be accused of peddling magic rather than enlisting disciples. It's the difference between a quick fix and "a long obedience in the same direction."[4]

An "Answerizing" Church

If not closely reined in, "the answer" tradition can enlarge its field of reference so that it's not just Jesus who is being championed; it is all manner of answers to vexing issues that now have "Christian" answers. Greg Jones, former Dean of Duke Divinity School, introduced me to a made-up word for the practice of spewing such unreflective, formulaic "Christian" replies to sincere questions. That word is *answerizing.* "Answerizing" allows you to give The One Correct Answer, typically a buzzword or cliché that neatly dodges the complexity or pain of a question while appearing to deal with it. Politicians, radio talk-show gurus, and television talking heads are especially good at "answerizing." So are some church folks.

In *Souls Raised from the Dead,* novelist Doris Betts offers us a portrait of an "answerizing" clergyman: the fictional character Reverend Billy Ware. We meet him when he arrives at a hospital waiting room to visit the family of a girl who suffers from acute renal failure. The father of the hospitalized girl, Frank, sees the pastor emerging from the hospital elevator and attempts a hasty but impossible departure from the waiting room. So he stiffly greets the clergyman, noting his serene look. "One reason Billy Ware looked so serene was that he was deaf," writes Betts. "It wasn't much of an occupational hazard, Frank supposed, for a man who could respond to anything by quoting Scripture." As Billy Ware converses with the family, we learn he has one hearing aid to assist him when he is listening to parishioners like Frank and his mother, but "in the pulpit . . . he wore hearing aids in *both* ears."[5] So what is most important? Really hearing what others are saying or being avidly attuned to one's own voice?

If Billy Ware's self-infatuation is sadly comedic, Sam Harris, a noted atheist author and lecturer, offers a less comedic assessment of how "answerizing" strikes outsiders. Harris marvels over "the frequency with which people of faith praise themselves for their humility, while condemning scientists and other nonbelievers for their intellectual arrogance." He is referring to the belief that scientists and intellectuals supposedly know more than all lower life forms— or at least pretend to. In Harris's estimation, however, "an average Christian, in an average church, listening to an average Sunday sermon has achieved a level of arrogance simply unimaginable in scientific discourse—and there have been some extraordinarily arrogant scientists."[6]

What happens to a society when the church prefers the sound of its own voice to compassionate listening as others share their thoughts? I think it's demonstrable in the abundance of Broadway and Hollywood productions that portray persons dealing with excruciating dilemmas without any faith resources. They typically wrestle alone, stoically, and if church or faith is brought into the story, it is in the form of a whiskey priest or a dim-witted preacher or an infuriating self-righteous biddy—all stock personifications of the dead-end street named Religion. Whatever the church might have to offer is peremptorily dismissed as irrelevant, insulting, and repugnant. The "answerizing" church has been tried and found wanting in popular culture.

A Choir of Questioners

Fortunately, our day is also distinguished by an increasing cry—among church people themselves!—for a faith and for a church that speaks and acts with more depth, more humility, and certainly more sensitivity. This cry is global, consistent, and growing.

• German Protestant theologian Heinz Zahrnt lamented that the church in 1970s Germany was speaking with exclamation points rather than question marks and hurling its answers at people's heads like meteors from a distant star. The principal virtue it preached was obedience, rather than thinking for oneself. The sadness of this practice, he said, was made all the more tragic by the fact that the church was mostly answering questions no one was asking.[7]

• Japanese Christian missionary-theologian Kosuke Koyama expressed his frustration as one who had been on the receiving end of the church's answer-laden missionary enterprise. He charged the church in Asia with having a teacher complex, being "most interested in teaching people, but not interested in being taught by people. It speaks to people, but it does not listen to them. I do not think Christianity in Asia for the last 400 years has really listened to the people."[8]

• Bono, the Irish rock star and unapologetic born-again Christian, was asked how he could release a song like "I Still Haven't Found What I'm Looking For." He replied, "Being a Christian hasn't given me all the answers; instead it's given me a whole new set of questions."[9]

• Isaac Slade, the lead singer-pianist of the rock band The Fray (as in "above the fray"), is representative of a younger generation of American Christians. Although all the band's members grew up in conservative Christian homes and consider their music to be spiritual, he says, "We don't call ourselves a Christian band. Because when you get into marketing, 'Christian' means that you have everything together, and you're always happy, and you want everybody to start coming to your church. The common denominators in the music I've liked [are] the honesty of not having answers and the passion to find them. I think that's what spiritual music has, whether it's Christian or pop or new age."[10]

• Emergent church author Brian McLaren says that in the emerging postmodern culture of the twenty-first century, "[the church's] greatest enemy will not be our ignorance; it will be our unteachability. It won't be what we don't know that threatens us; it will be what we do know. We know too much—so much that we can't learn how much we need to learn."[11]

• Even Pope Francis, Roman Catholicism's surprising twenty-first-century leader, says that if someone has all the answers, "that is proof that God is not with him." The great leaders of the faith, Francis declares, have always left room for uncertainty. "You must leave room for the Lord, not for our certainties."[12]

These are but a small representation of the many voices calling for a church and a faith that, while not lacking answers, seeks understanding as much as it seeks the microphone, that listens receptively to the questions before it attempts to reply, that invites interrogation from others as an essential component of its own witness, that is as open to learn from and be taught by the questioner as it is to utter its answers.

These voices ask for the recognition that the twenty-first-century world is in many ways a different place from the world known to our forebears. Faiths that once were foreign curiosities are now next-door neighbors. Values that were once assumed to be universal are now perceived to be regional and of recent birth. Questions once thought to be settled are now being reopened or asked quite differently.

These voices, both within and outside the church, ask the church to admit candidly that she also "walks by faith and not by sight" (2 Cor 5:7), that absolute certainty is not the same thing as faith-anchored assurance, and that some dilemmas don't have "answers"—they more properly have faith-*full* or faith-*less* responses.

Convincing Questions?

Heinz Zahrnt, the German theologian quoted above, suggested that the church follow a cue given by Bertolt Brecht in a tale he titled "Convincing Questions." An ideological leader in Brecht's story says, "I have noticed that we frighten many people away from our teaching by having an answer to everything. Could we not, in the interests of propaganda, draw up a list of questions, which seem to us completely unsolved?"

Zahrnt, cueing from Brecht's line, pled for a German church that would, not in the interests of propaganda but in faithfulness to the gospel, listen to the completely unsolved questions asked by the people. The church leaders would be sworn to dialogue honestly with these "convincing questions" and to do so not just as clever deceivers playing dumb, but as humble yet believing "conductors of the choir of questioners."[13]

Zahrnt's proposal isn't as odd as it may first appear. Jesus grew up among a people, Israel, who can legitimately be characterized as the conductor of earth's choir of questioners. And, as this book seeks to show, Jesus learned from and masterfully practiced the question methodology in his own ministry. He followed the pattern he'd observed within the holy writings taught him from childhood, the writings known popularly to Christians as the Old Testament. Page after page of these Hebrew Scriptures is sprinkled with memorable questions, each one representative of Israel's ages-long dialogue with God. They begin as early as the opening chapters of the first book. In the Garden of Eden, God asks Adam, "Where are you?" (Gen 3:9). In the following chapter, God asks murderous Cain, "Where is your brother?" and receives a question in reply: "Am I my brother's keeper?" (Gen 4:9). Is not the whole drama of life captured in those three questions? But there is much more. There is besieged Job's cry to God: "If mortals die, will they live again?" (Job 14:14). There is the psalmist's astonished question, "What are human beings that you [God] are mindful of them?" (Ps 8:4), and there is the anguished question of God evoked by that very mindfulness: "What more was there to do for my vineyard that I have not done in it?" (Isa 5:4). Even the commandments of God can be stated in the interrogative rather than the imperative mood, as the prophet Micah demonstrated in his famous summary: "What does the LORD require of you but to do justice, and to love kindness, and to walk humbly with your God?" (Mic 6:8). The entire book of Ecclesiastes, on the other hand, offers the questioning of one who finds conventional answers of faith awkward if not incredible, and Israel chose to enshrine this counter-testimony within its holy writings.

Israel was and is above all else a dialogue partner with Yahweh, a listener and also a questioner walking with God through the centuries. Her very name, Israel, has the literal meaning of "one who struggles with God" (Gen 32:28). All of her canonically deposited questions— far exceeding in number the sample cited above—established the precedent and basis for a later Judaism that never saw a compelling need (or way!) to construct doctrinal statements comparable to Christianity's many creeds. In the twelfth century, Moses Maimonides did offer a summation of Judaism in thirteen articles of faith, which some later Jewish prayer books printed with the introductory creedal phrase, "I firmly believe that . . . ."[14] But Maimonides' creed was never widely followed. Instead, the Jewish faith has been sustained across the centuries by the slimmest of credos, known as the *Shema* ("Hear, O Israel: The LORD is our God, the LORD alone. You shall love the LORD your God with all your heart, and with all your soul, and with all your might," Deut 6:4-5), by its thoughtful, history-shaped traditions, and by its treasury of biblical stories that have been lovingly rehearsed and explored and endlessly questioned by generation after generation. So characteristic is the Jewish appreciation for provocative questions that there are countless stories about it. A favorite of mine tells of an exasperated student who asks his rabbi why he never answers his disciples' questions directly, but always replies with another question. The rabbi replies, "So what is wrong with a question?"

Frank Luntz, the well-known wordsmith whose services are currently sought by politicians and advertisers alike, says that one of the ten rules of effective language use is "Ask a Question." He says that communicators must remember that "sometimes it's not what you *say* but what you *ask* that really matters," and he adds that "a statement, when put in the form of a rhetorical question, can have much greater impact than a plain assertion."

Luntz contends that if a speaker simply asserts something, the response depends to some degree on the listener's opinion of the speaker. But expressing the same statement in the form of a question invites personal involvement. Thus, the use of a well-wrought question places the idea within the listener's consciousness even if the listener dislikes or distrusts the questioner.[15]

The Stranger who Knows How to Ask Questions

Jesus of Nazareth clearly stands in the great Jewish tradition of asking "convincing questions." Though Christians comb through the Gospels for Jesus' statements as a foundation for their answers, even his statements were often indirect, or offered in subtle and multivalent parables—or dangled in mid-air as stunning questions. His disciples are often depicted as dull-witted students bumbling around in confusion and trying to understand what their master has just said. Mark's Gospel is especially adept at this portrayal, but it is the Gospel of John that uses Jesus' own puzzling speech as a primary literary device to propel further elucidation. The Savior presented by John is a master in using words and terms that were always open to multiple meanings, prompting at least one group of impatient listeners to challenge Jesus to "tell us plainly" what his meaning was (John 10:24). Is it not fitting, therefore, to insist that the church that esteems Jesus as "the way, the truth, and the life" (John 14:6) also value him just as fruitfully and biblically as a "conductor of the choir of questioners"?

Admittedly, considering Jesus as a Jewish teacher who asked questions and who taught (and teaches) in the rabbi's interrogatory mode is unexplored territory for many. We are far more accustomed to noting his deeds and quoting his pronouncements. This is demonstrable by how often the publishers of Bibles add somewhere a listing of Jesus' miracles or an index to his statements about various subjects. But I've yet to find a Bible that includes a listing of his questions.

Perhaps the absence of such a list is because there are so many of them—140 or so separate questions by my rough count!—depending on whether or not you count duplicate accounts within the four Gospels. Oddly, even though the Gospels include these questions as faithfully as any miracle or parable, our eyes have been so trained by our answer-laden tradition that we routinely skip his questions in order to get to the better-known "good stuff."

How foolish! Jesus has so much to say to us through his questions. Many of them, admittedly, are only conversational and thus not exactly revelatory. But others seem to linger in our consciousness, waiting for a response—a response that Jesus doesn't supply. We usually call these rhetorical questions and dismiss them as verbal set-ups. But, heeding the observation of Frank Luntz that rhetorical questions open a conversation, I think Jesus' so-called rhetorical questions remain on the page not just to report long-ago conversations but also to invite a conversation between Jesus and readers through the centuries. In my experience, it's been Jesus' questions that have often challenged my easy answers and sent me out with new questions.

When studying Jesus' parables or even his miracles, we often need help to understand the significance of what is being said or done. Jesus' questions, however, seem to leap across the ages, freed from historical context and needing little scholarly interpretation to help us "get it." His questions are what they are: enduring inquiries about substantive matters that invite response, inquiries not bound to the circumstances of their origin. They are a special form of Jesus' lingering presence with us, nudging listeners to thoughtful reflection in every age.

The same might be said of all his sayings, of course, but it's especially so with these rhetorical questions of Jesus. They can lead each reader/hearer into the thickest forests of soul work. When listened to and taken to heart, the questions are as enlightening and explosive as any pronouncement or parable; perhaps they are even more so because the answers one ponders aren't filched from the next sentence or paragraph on the page but from what is written and being written in the hidden crannies of the heart where spirit meets with Spirit.

When we allow these questions to sink in, our attitudes begin to shift. We feel ourselves in dialogue with a Person, not just kicking around a philosophical concept. And, answering that Person, we may be shocked by what comes out of our mouths or minds, and then spend days dealing with the fact that it actually came from places deeper within. The good, the bad, the whimpering—as well as the altogether lovely—come tumbling out, and then we either have to mop it up or polish it.

Not least of all, using Jesus' questions as a learning device curtails the zealot's uncritical adoption of a direct statement as the "final answer." Direct statements can become the ammunition for crusades. Questions, on the other hand, foster reflection and thoughtfulness. They pry the cudgel of proof-texts from our hands and encourage us to look again—and to look within. Faith's profession isn't thereby forfeited, but its utterance now comes from deeper places and broader sympathies. The church that emerges from such reflection can walk more humbly with its God, itself, and its neighbors. "Answerizing" is no longer its mode of being—or at least that's the hope I bring to this project.

Perhaps it is disingenuous of me to use the questions of *Jesus* rather than the questions of the *world* as the format for the conversation we are beginning. After all, I have made a big deal of our need to listen to the world's questions. I could have identified some of those questions as the topics for this book, but my operating hunch is that we'll not become any better at hearing the questions of the often-ignored world if we fail to listen to the questions of the Christ we profess to worship. Attentiveness to them and attentiveness to him are linked. His questions, in fact, consistently address the very issues with which we and our world are wrestling. But his questions go deeper, providing help even as they prompt us to further reflection.

The process of learning, unlearning, and relearning must begin somewhere. So my choice is to begin with Jesus as the first voice to consider. My hope is that this means our ears and hearts will actually hear through him the cries of the world, and that we in turn will re-enroll ourselves in the learners' class and be readied to offer him and the world the more faithful responses that both deserve.

"What You Ask Really Matters"

In the following pages I invite you to find your place around a seaside campfire or lean against the stone wall of a village synagogue and listen with me to some of Jesus' questions—and, of course, to my replies. I'm not delusional enough to think I've given the best responses, or even good responses. These are just my responses, and what I hope you hear in the following pages is the stammering of one believer at one point in his life. I've tried to listen to what Jesus asked—and to pay attention to what his words stir up in me and where they take me—and to report this as clearly as I can. My purpose isn't to solicit your "Yes!" to my responses; it's to prompt your own meditations and replies to these enduring questions. Jesus is your true conversation partner, not I.

Two confessions: First, I haven't selected easy questions. I have chosen some that I believe echo the world's deepest questions, inquiries I consider to be timely as well as timeless. Each is high-octane material, so I'll be surprised if your responses match mine. Second, as you may already suspect, as you read you'll be eavesdropping on the ruminations of a "cut-and-run" listener. While I worked on this project, there were many days when I found the heat of Jesus' questions uncomfortable. So the next day—or even months—I didn't even show up to listen to "the Stranger who knows how to ask questions." Instead, I just walked away from his probing and found a cooler, shadier place to do my living. More often than not, my chosen shade became darkness, and then, in spite of his heat, his light drew me back. This too is a fascinating dimension of Jesus: he's never pushy. But then he's also never boring and never, ever easily silenced. If you doubt that, just ask the folks who tried to silence him twenty centuries ago.

NOTES

1. B. B. McKinney, "Satisfied with Jesus," *The Broadman Hymnal* (Nashville: Broadman Press, 1940) 375.

2. See, for example, Martin Heidegger, *Discourses on Thinking* (Harper Torchbooks, 1969) and Ludwig Wittgenstein, *Tractatus Logico-Philosophicus*, trans. C. K. Ogden (New York: Dover Publications, 1998).

3. Andraé Crouch, "Jesus Is the Answer," *Live at Carnegie Hall*, Light Records, 1973. Michael W. Smith recorded this song in 1996 for *Tribute: The Songs of Andraé Crouch*, produced by Warner Brothers.

4. Eugene Peterson brought this phrase to popular attention through his book *A Long Obedience in the Same Direction: Discipleship in an Instant Society* (Downers Grove IL: Intervarsity Press, 1980) although, as Peterson notes, the phrase is from Friedrich Nietzsche.

5. Doris Betts, *Souls Raised from the Dead* (New York: Alfred A. Knopf, 1994) 170, emphasis added.

6. Sam Harris, *Letter to a Christian Nation* (New York: Alfred A. Knopf, 2006) 74–75.

7. Heinz Zahrnt, *What Kind of God? A Question of Faith*, trans. R. A. Wilson (Minneapolis: Augsburg Publishing House, 1972) 84ff.

8. Kosuke Koyama, "Christianity Suffers from 'Teacher Complex,'" *Evangelization*, vol. 2 of *Mission Trends*, ed. Gerald H. Anderson and Thomas F. Starnsky (Grand Rapids MI: Eerdmans Publishing, 1975) 71–72.

9. Bono, cited in Tony Campolo, *Speaking My Mind* (Nashville: W Group, 2004) xii.

10. Elysa Gardner, "Debut 'How to Save a Life' Takes on a Life of Its Own," *USA Today*, 13 July 2006, D4, online at http://usatoday30.usatoday.com /life/music/news/2006-07-12-otv-the-fray_x.htm.

11. Brian McLaren, *The Church on the Other Side: Doing Ministry in the Postmodern Matrix* (Grand Rapids MI: Zondervan, 2005) 38–39.

12. Pope Francis, *America,* 30 September 2013, cited in "Century Marks," *Christian Century* (16 October 2013): 8.

13. Zahrnt, *What Kind of God?*, 88.

14. Abraham Joshua Heschel, *God in Search of Man: A Philosophy of Judaism* (New York: Harper Torchbook, 1966) 21.

15. Frank Luntz, *Words that Work: It's Not What You Say, It's What People Hear* (New York: Hyperion, 2007) 23–25, emphasis added.

Chapter 2

A Question about Value

"Are you not of more value than they?" (Matthew 6:26)

The "birds of the air" are the "they" in this question. Apparently, "they" were as easily overlooked by most of the people of Jesus' day as they are in ours. The only time many of us notice birds is when they startle us with an unexpected chirp or leave an unwanted calling card on the polished surfaces of our cars. Birds of the air. Other than that fraction of the populace who bird watch, who pays attention to them?

Well, according to Jesus, God does. Birds are of value to God, their maker. In another place, Jesus is said to have claimed that God actually takes note of the fall of each sparrow (Matt 10:29), a claim that is as mind-boggling to me as it likely is heartening to members of the Audubon Society.

Unfortunately, I've also read that as many as 80 percent of some species of birds die every winter due to the extremes of their habitat. Have you seen a fallen bird, lying frozen on a city sidewalk? Or a wounded one, the victim of a car or truck, fluttering on the highway's surface? In a nanosecond, it's just road kill, a momentary greasy target for uncaring Michelins rolling down the interstate. It's not a pretty picture—even for a God who has seen it all.

Still, Jesus believes God is looking out for these birds. And, to be fair, the amazing, species-perpetuating migration habits of many of them do supply some evidence for Jesus' belief. Add the fact that these little creatures survive "in the raw" century after century, finding food and water even when the earth seems like a frozen or arid wasteland, and that's got to count as some kind of argument for a preserving power at work. Jesus understands it to be God's kind of power, and he obviously believes that God's kind of power has an even keener interest in the welfare of humans. Hence, his question: "Are you not of more value [to God] than they?"

It is a question we continue to raise with grief-filled urgency, for our world is filled with grisly stories of earthquakes, tsunamis, terrorist attacks, genocides, and school murders that surely don't bolster belief in an observant, valuing Deity. For that matter, our Western world is also filled with nursing homes populated by residents whose golden years are often brutally gray. These expensive storage bins that await the elderly seldom provide proof that there's a God who is looking out for us.

If we want to get pushy about it, we could even cite the Bible itself, whole pages of which are filled with accounts of people who were slaughtered because, according to the text, God *ordered* their destruction. Of course, as some are quick to point out, the Bible's slaughtered are usually people of the "wrong" faith or practices or clan—they are supposedly "the bad guys" who had it coming. To such thinking I can only reply that if God actually authorized such cleansings, then we have more trouble on our hands than I know how to process. I choose to believe that God's will is misreported in these stories even though I know the Bible itself doesn't disown the statements or spend one paragraph doctoring God's résumé. (That is, unless one believes God eventually answered those biblical reports of Divine holocausts by undergoing one himself—at Golgotha.)

Historians say that in Jesus' lifetime, the occupying Roman soldiers sometimes decorated stretches of Judean roadways with the crosses of crucified troublemakers whose exposed bodies were left aloft as public examples, becoming carrion for these very "birds of the air" Jesus is so sure God cares about. Surely Jesus and his listeners weren't blind; they had witnessed these "road signs"! Nonetheless, he spoke to them of a caring God, and they listened without laughing at him.

How am I to respond to the question, "Are you not of more value than the birds of the air?" Perhaps one place to begin is to admit that if I believe, as one gospel song declares, that "his eye is on the sparrow, and I know he watches me," it's because I've chosen faith over knowledge.[1]

There is a difference between believing and knowing, a difference that's often blurred, as though faith were just another name for religious knowledge. In fact, faith is the word for convictions whose truth we will never *know* until this life is over. Knowledge has to do with data and broadly acknowledged truth, with statements like, "Martin Luther King Jr. was murdered in Memphis, Tennessee." Consequently, faith and knowledge can't helpfully be talked about as though they were two sides of one coin.[2] To talk of faith and knowledge is like talking about crab cakes and European history, two very different things. Both are real, and each good in its own way, but you don't want to confuse the two—especially if you are hungry.

Thus I must reply to Jesus' question about our value that God's affirmation of the value of human life is a statement of faith and not of knowledge. There's too much knowledge of the cheapness of human life and too much knowledge of the silence of heaven to be able to say, "I *know* God cares for us." Even though we can't honestly say that, faith can enter a counterclaim and profess, "I nonetheless *believe* God does care, and values us dearly."

People who say "I believe" are choosing to speak in defiance of observable, contradictory evidence. They are, in fact, engaging in the very kind of protest speech that fills the Bible's pages. Consider just one example of this appearance-defying kind of speech:

Happy are those whose help is the God of Jacob,
whose hope is in the LORD their God,
who made heaven and earth,
the sea and all that is in them;
who keeps faith forever;
who executes justice for the oppressed;
who gives food to the hungry.

The LORD sets the prisoners free;
the LORD opens the eyes of the blind.
The LORD lifts up those who are bowed down;
the LORD loves the righteous.
The LORD watches over the strangers;
he upholds the orphan and the widow,

but the way of the wicked he brings to ruin.
The LORD will reign forever,
your God, O Zion, for all generations.
Praise the LORD! (Ps 146:5-10)

This is typical of the joyful song of believing people through the ages, and its chief characteristic is that it repeatedly affirms a caring intervention that's not always evident. It is a song only faith can sing, realizing that there's a counter-melody simultaneously moaned by the parched lips and empty stares of the starving.

At the same time, we must give full credit for those occasions—innumerable throughout history—when "something" happened that can only be called miraculous. The illness relented, the inevitable calamity didn't come, the people were freed, the storm passed. It's possible that the song cited above was originally a thanksgiving song composed after just such an occasion and later generalized upon as though happy outcomes were the unbroken rule. In any event, wonderful surprises *do* happen, and we would be ignoring those if we conclude that "believing the best" is unforgivably stupid and a denial of reality. There is indeed a stout case to be made for those who choose to join the Bible's believing protest speech and affirm that "happy are those whose help is the God of Jacob."

Hence, Jesus' question really does put a choice before us. Will we interpret our existence by faith, or will we interpret it by knowledge? Will we live as people who trust that a Caring Center is at work in often invisible ways, or will we live as people who are content to accept that what we see is all there is? It's certainly not a slam-dunk for either side of the proposition. Jesus, despite his many statements regarding the reality of the invisible, drops the entire matter into our laps with a question mark: "Are you not of more value . . . ?" The effect of that strategy is to put the matter squarely and personally before each of us: "Do I believe that we are actually of more value to God than birds or mosquitoes or pollywogs or the countless other living things that seem to live and die without even one little finger of God raised in apparent protest or aid?"

Who can say how any of us ever fall on the affirmative side of that huge question? Maybe it comes down to a choice of what kind of world we want to live in. A world without a Caring Center or a world with at least the possibility of one?

Suppose your answer is no; you do *not* believe you are of more value to God than the birds. If that's the case, nobody can fairly accuse you of being a rosy-minded simpleton or of having a spineless spirit that claims comfort at the expense of apparent truth. If you say no, you also settle a fundamental question about your way of life: you won't be one who is looking for help from elsewhere, be it from Above or from a divinely prompted neighbor. You're going to have a lively lookout for yourself, and most likely you will also keep a wary eye on others, expecting them to be similarly self-protective. That's not to say you'll be a mean, bad person. It's just to say that you'll live as one who isn't expecting to receive any breaks or feeling obliged to give any. Yours will be an "every man for himself" orientation.

On the other hand, suppose your answer is yes. There is surely a great comfort to be experienced as a consequence of such belief, even if it's based only on a wish. Many can tell stories of how faith in God's care sustained them when no other hope could be held—and of the anguish as they waited to see it. Many can go on to tell how, in the least promising circumstances, the longed-for help materialized in forms and through persons unimaginable. So, just like the naysayers, the answer to the question defines the life of the "yaysayers." A yes answer has a way of tying you to the Caring Center *and* to others in need.

This may, in fact, be the unexpected wallop within the question. You can't affirm God's valuing for yourself alone. If I dare to claim this belief as applicable to myself, it must be a belief that extends to all people—or else I am the most illogical as well as the most selfish of individuals, claiming for myself special rankings unavailable to others. If we say there is a God who has an active interest in our own well-being, then that belief amounts to more than a security blanket; it amounts to marching orders.

If you choose to say yes to this question, the world's pain becomes a call to care. That caring may be as quiet as a monetary gift to the beggar or the disaster victim, or a word of witness shared with an unbeliever. Or it may be as noisy as protesting war or racial discrimination, or as public as visiting and providing care for senior citizens or practicing greater care of Earth's resources, including its birds! Adolf Hitler built concentration camps and gas ovens as evidence of his faith in the valuing of certain kinds of people. Jesus' question makes me ask "What evidence exists to demonstrate my belief that *all* people count?"

It's almost a certainty that every human will one day feel as abandoned as Jesus did when he prayed, "My God, my God, why have you forsaken me?" What will matter most at that moment won't be what we *know* about the results of the CT scan or the ruling of the court or the migratory habits of birds, or any other knowing. In those moments, what will matter most is what we *believe* about the One who is reputedly creation's Caring Center.

At its heart, I think this question eventually becomes a question about the resurrection of Jesus. Both faith and knowledge can agree that he was crucified—an event that offers a disappointing demonstration of an uncaring world and an apparently silent, uncaring God. If Jesus' story ends on that Friday, so does the possibility of faith. But if the story resumes with an astonishing Sunday morning veto of Friday's atrocity, then faith's possibility is given new ground. An empty tomb opens the door to faith. Easter makes it possible to believe in a caring God.

Ready or not, life happens, and sometimes it ruthlessly forces us to act on one side or the other of Jesus' question, even if we'd rather not. A believing friend of mine lost a precocious eight-year-old daughter in a tornado. She concludes her story of that loss by saying it is important to "learn the songs before midnight." She is referring to the biblical story of the earliest Christian missionaries, Paul and Silas, who at the midnight hour sang songs of faith from the bowels of a Roman dungeon. Their backs were a bloody pulp from brutal Roman floggings, but their tongues were filled with the songs of consoling faith, songs they'd learned earlier, in easier hours. My friend says that had she not learned her own songs before her midnight hour, her daughter's death would have been even more devastating than it was. Her story pushes me to the realization that this choice between yes or no isn't one to postpone until someday, when we may want to have an opinion on the subject. Life is being made up—or lost—each passing minute.

Jesus, when I let myself think about the suffering endured all over the world, especially when I try to console friends who are enduring the most inexplicable trials, it's not always easy to believe that "somebody up there" knows or cares. But I believe you believed it, and I believe you went to a cross believing it. The fact that I'm talking to you now, as though you are still alive, is an indication that maybe, just maybe, there is One who in mysterious ways is still turning things right side up. If my maybe is in truth a reality, please nurture it within me—and in all who struggle to believe and hope. Amen.

NOTES

1. "His Eye Is on the Sparrow," words by Civilla D. Martin, music by Charles H. Gabriel, 1905.

2. This is not to say that faith does not lead to its own kind of knowing. Indeed, the knowledge that comes through faith is often richer than that found within data and information, per se. Nonetheless, for this discussion, it is essential to emphasize the difference between these two.

Chapter 3

A Question about Self-understanding

"Why do you see the speck in your neighbor's eye, but do not notice the log in your own eye?" (Matthew 7:3)

It is said that human nature never changes, and that's probably true. I can't be too dogmatic, however, about what people were like thousands of years ago. For instance, we're told that the Bible's King David once "danced before the LORD with all his might" (2 Sam 6:14). Apparently, in doing so, his "private parts" were also on display—and not only to the Lord! It wasn't one of David's most dignified, regal moments. When he returned home, Queen Michal unloaded on him for "uncovering himself . . . as any vulgar fellow might." She had a point, to be certain. But when you read the story of the whole relationship between these two, you have to wonder if she had any idea of what she had become. Did it cross her mind that her soured-up stateliness wasn't something others ought to behold any more than David's nakedness? That perhaps she was displaying things that could use covering up? Apparently not. So, based on this story and a passel of other ancient stories like it, I'm prepared to think that the pickiness problem raised in Jesus' question has been with us for a long, long time.

Maybe the originator of this pickiness problem, this marriage of self-excusing and other-judging, was actually Adam, when he tried to make God believe that the *tiny* drip of apple juice on his lip was actually Eve's *big* fault. When you're trying to wiggle off the hook, fractions become all important! The fact that Jesus, centuries later, elevates the issue via this question certifies that the problem was alive and well long after Adam's day. It still thrives.

Like many folks, I have a bedroom in my house that I've adapted into an office. If you're brave enough to open its door and attempt to enter, you'll walk into mounds of clippings and stacks of old magazines and books and other "stuff I'm going to get around to someday." Long ago, my wife and I agreed that this room would be my lair, my haven, my nest to muss up—and to clean up. Consequently, I don't remember the last time its blinds were dusted or its carpet vacuumed. Sure, that spider and cobweb up in the northwest corner is unquestionably off-putting, and the coffee stains on the throw rug are ugly. But it's *my* clutter, *my* cobweb, *my* stain, and *my* room, and therefore it's no big deal.

Given this personal messiness, you might think I'd be similarly tolerant of clutter in the remainder of the house. But that's not so. If dirty dishes pile up in the kitchen, I get sullen. If the living areas of the house are cluttered and remain so for more than a day, I become a grouch, irked that my wife (who's obviously the God-designated cleaner-upper in this house!) isn't maintaining our home in a hygienic and esthetically acceptable state.

Now, lest I leave you with the impression that she is the Sanitation Department's worst nightmare, let me quickly add that she is a good housekeeper. Most days you could drop in on us unannounced and not want to ask for the Pine Sol. But still, she doesn't notice a lot of things, important things, like the fact that the canned vegetables in the pantry aren't arranged in alphabetical order, or that the To Be Paid bills on the kitchen counter, awaiting my check-writing, aren't stacked by sequential due date and with the lower left corners of the envelopes aligned. It's a most impossible situation for me, an altogether sweet, gentle, gracious, and rational man, "practically perfect in every way," to live with a woman who's so untidy!

Now, if I have stretched the truth a mite here—actually by many miles!—the painful reality is that we have had more icy words over this pickiness/neatness issue than over anything else in our most gratifying marriage. To this day, I still find it much easier to groan over *her* dirty dishes than even to notice the fat spider swaying on the web in *my* office. With that being admitted, I'm willing to bet the price of a full month of Molly Maid cleaning service that ours isn't the only home that's stalked by the demon of pickiness, of people who are blind to their own flaws but have perfect vision in detecting and announcing the flaws of others.

This problem of "speck-obsession" is troublesome enough on the interpersonal level, but it extends into broader areas. While I certainly do not intend to label the events of September 11, 2001, as being "a speck," I must note that in the post 9-11 days, one of the better questions some Americans raised was, "Why do they hate us so?" The deep, unspeakable question struggling to find its way to some lips was something like this: "Why would anyone do this to us? How on earth could Americans and American life be so offensive as to provoke such a hideous act against us?"

That event was one of the rare moments when many of us were stunned enough to consider the possibility of looking in the mirror. But this daring thought was immediately squelched by those who said that using the event as a call to self-examination was a despicably unpatriotic response, a treasonous attempt to portray us as villains rather than victims. "How dare you reframe this event as being in any way our fault?" they asked. "No! There is nothing wrong with America other than our mollycoddling of these extremists for far too long." America's opportunity for self-reflection was angrily rejected as unpatriotic. Our vision of others' errors was declared to be flawless, while our momentary willingness to look in the mirror was rebuffed.

Of course, there's nothing uniquely American about this reaction. I understand that in some Japanese presentations of World War II, the attack on Pearl Harbor is explained as an inevitable and justified response to Western imperialism—not anything like a sneak attack on a non-combatant nation. We may safely assume that from the beginning of time, this is the way conflicts and wars have been launched, explained, and defended before the world.

Robert Cormier has artfully described some other expressions of the same "we versus them" dynamic in our daily assessments. He observes,

> When we don't dress, we go Casual. But when they don't dress, they're slobs.

Our house has character—theirs is rundown.

Or, our house has that lived-in look—their house looks worn out.

We are slender—but they are skinny.

We have been putting on a little weight lately, but they are getting fat.

They have terrorists—we have freedom fighters.

They are moralistic—we are moral.

They are reactionary—we are traditional.

They are racist—we want to preserve our identity.

Our friend hasn't been feeling well for some time—their friend is a hypochondriac.

Our children are inquisitive—their children are nosy.[1]

Jesus asks, "Why do you act like this?" It's a great question. But before it's a question, it's actually a declaration, isn't it? Being more critical of others than of ourselves is an unconscious habit, a way of navigating through life that goes unchallenged far too often. Jesus, however, challenges us. He refuses to leave us anchored in the safe harbor of our unconscious behavioral patterns. He brings our failure to judge ourselves and others fairly into the light bluntly, pointedly—as though everyone within earshot has this issue, acknowledged or not. Rack up ten points for Jesus' reading of human nature. The man knows what questions to ask!

Indeed, what causes us to be so critical of others, so observant of their failures, but often so belligerently defensive of our own flaws? This question leads us to the deep end of the theologians' pool of ideas about sin or to scary plunges into Freudian depth analysis. But before taking these cerebral escape hatches, here's a more down-home reply—my own immediate, ground-level, semi-serious reply to Jesus' great question.

(I'm giving myself permission to continue to horse around with this question for a moment, even though the issue is deadly serious. But can anyone believe Jesus didn't have a grin on his face or anticipate smiles to appear on the faces of his listeners when he talked about a two-by-four protruding from the eye of a sawdust-speck remover?)

Here then is my cut-to-the-chase answer: The reason we can so easily detect others' errors is because there's such an appalling number of jerks in the world. Face it. For every nice-smelling, housebroken, well-integrated person you meet, there are twenty whose prickly, rude behavior and egotistic or political or religious repulsiveness are off the chart. Some days it seems that the number of emotionally healthy, pleasant people in the world is shrinking faster than the ozone layer. Surely it's only a matter of time before some Gallup poll will sustain me in this conclusion.

For instance, consider the likelihood that 70 percent of the people who attend family reunions each year really don't want to—and it's not because these events are often held in locations where only mosquitoes or cactus thrive or where a cup of coffee costs five dollars. We don't want to go because of the embarrassing people who show up at these events. It's Aunt Myrtle who wears way too much perfume and Cousin Bill with his loud, corny jokes and Nephew Artis with his latest and most bizarre "significant other." Not to mention Great Aunt Sallie who always distributes her unsold Avon products as gifts for everyone in attendance—and rewards the one who's traveled farthest with the latest version of Soap-on-a-Rope!

But these people are your family. You are bone of their bone and flesh of their flesh. Which is, of course, utterly humiliating. And that, it seems to me, is probably the point buried within Jesus' question.

We are all one family, one big, messed-up, dysfunctional family. Whether our family name happens to be Smith or Ekweku or Zawahiri or Grunewald or Carreras. Whether our skin pigmentation happens to be pale or dark or a mixture thereof, or whether our native tongue is Indo-European or Slavic, Swahili or Semitic. As the Scripture says metaphorically, and the geneticists declare empirically, we are all "made of one blood" (Acts 17:26, KJV). We are the one family of humankind, and all of us are up to our armpits in grieving, loving, conniving, mending, killing, forgetting, cherishing, denying, clutching, fighting—and dying. Driven by histories we never fully fathom and drawn by dreams we seldom ever attain, we live in spasms, one leg limping away from *x,* the other thrashing wildly toward *y.* Who can comprehend our odyssey? But this is who we are, and no one—no one!—escapes the woundedness of the family connection.

Only when I forget my own family connectedness, only when I deny my permanent membership in this human incompleteness can I be hypercritical of another. Sure, I can do it. I do it all too often, only to discover eventually how lonely it is up there in the error-free zone of my self-declared superiority.

So when I grumble about how many jerks there are in the world, I trust you realize what an arrogant and impossible turf is being defended. I'm exempting myself from the human race, playing a losing game of solo exceptionalism and possibly even issuing a covert invitation for you to join my elitist purity party. But it's an invitation you'll be wise to decline. Eventually, you too will disappoint me, and I'll dump you for some infraction, even if nothing more than your underwear is showing (as with King David).

A more adequate and honest answer to Jesus' question about the pattern of cutting down others might begin with the admission that it has something to do with our rejection of family. We don't want to admit that the family's fouled-up DNA courses through our veins and fills our fiber. In truth, it's not just others we don't like; it is ourselves. There's too much about our own selves that disappoints us—our shape, our color, our behavior, our hair, our intelligence, our face, our crowd, our bank balance, our accent, our plainness. Everyone is embarrassed about some facet—if not with the entirety—of themselves. But rather than admit that and deal with our own flaws, we zero in on what is dislikable in others and zap it and them. Instead of confronting "me" and handling "me," I make exceptions for "me" that I certainly don't make for "you," and, since I've turned my full attention to "you," I no longer have to deal with "me." No wonder "you" don't fare too well, while "I" soar in my self-designed popularity poll!

Still, even with a beam in one's eye, it's not that difficult, eventually, to see the trickery that's going on here. What *is* difficult, incredibly difficult, is to own up to how vicious this trait is. Although the Bible says "the root of all evil is in the love of money," I think that pronouncement ought to be supplemented by another statement: "the *tap*root of all evil is buried in our dislike of ourselves and of anything that reminds us of what garden-variety commoners we really are."

Now, if I'm anywhere close to the truth of why we are such consistent and lethal speck-spotters, the next question (which Jesus doesn't pose here, but his original question surely forces us to ask it) is this: Is there any way we can change this sick pattern?

I think so. We can't change it overnight or fix it permanently in ourselves or in others, but we can disrupt it, slow it down. If nothing more, simply facing the question and dealing with it honestly is a huge and essential first step in the change process. The something more that is needed, however, comes from beyond. And this is one of those times where Jesus is our Guide as well as the best Questioner.

Our great hope arises when we hear a word of grace coming from beyond, a word that enables us to say to one another, "You're not okay, but I'm not okay, either"—and even if that's not the cheerful truth we want to entertain, it opens us to hear the greater truth that ultimately our not-okayness *is* okay because God loves us, both of us, all of us, in spite of our flaws. I think this means that God remembers that ultimately we are simply dust. God is the one who put us together that way—dust-based carbon forms—and God is also the one who said in Golgotha-red ink that it's okay to be dust, to be who we are. God doesn't hold it against us, nor should we punish ourselves for being less than perfect.

Or, to put it in my earlier inelegant terminology, once we admit that we are members of Jerkdom and also realize that God has known this from the beginning and loved us anyway—even going the distance of joining us in our Jerkdom and dying to cover our sorry, self-centered track records—once we see this and own up to it, we don't need to spend our lives running away from our selves or picking others apart. We can begin to befriend our selves—warts and all—and befriend our misshapen brothers and sisters, and even our God! We can quit being civil wars and become maturing adults. Who knows, we may even find something enjoyable in Aunt Myrtle and Cousin Bill! (Well, maybe.)

Many years ago I led a weekly Bible study group for young mothers. This was before church women were bold enough to say out loud that they certainly didn't need a man to teach them about motherhood. But their warm inclusion made me feel like one of the girls, and the group became a marvelous experience in sharing the exasperations all of us endured as we tried to grow up while playing the part of being the grown-ups in our children's lives. Some hilarious yet painfully honest sharing and encouragement took place in that little circle of learners. When the group concluded its six-month run, Vicky, whose three preschoolers would have given me a nervous breakdown in a heartbeat, gave me a gift I still cherish. It's a small, decoupage plaque she fashioned on her kitchen table when she wasn't wiping runny noses or other anatomical areas. It bears this trenchant phrase: "Not to see through others, but to see others through."

When I get too critical of some imperfect fellow human, I try to remember Vicky's motto. I'd be lying if I said its counsel blinds me to the grotesque speck in another's eye (after all, it is wedged in there so disgustingly!), but I'm confident that it's sometimes kept me from dissecting him while this log is dangling from my left eye socket.

As for the political and international implications of this matter, I punt. I suppose it's too much to hope that the power people of the world will ever practice much critical self-awareness. Their need to believe the lie that all malignancy resides elsewhere is too overwhelming for them to admit otherwise. But if churches and religions and races and nations are incapable of dealing with this, it's all the more important for the individuals who do "get it" to truly get it, and to respect each member of the family—beginning with the people-in-process who are visible each morning in their mirrors.

Jesus, I've teased with this question of yours. Part of the reason is that I'm still trying to escape the self-confrontation your question demands. The truth is, I still have so many insecurities that in some way it feels good to pick others apart, imagining it will make me feel better about myself, will prove to me that I am as good as or better than they. It's never worked that well for me, but I keep trying. Is it possible there's a better way for me to feel okay about myself? Is it possible you can help me—all of us, actually—to feel all right enough about ourselves that we don't need to keep passing judgment on others? Amen.

NOTE

1. Robert Cormier, "I Have Words to Spend," cited in Greer, Colin, and Herbert Kohl, eds., *A Call to Character: A Family Treasury* (New York: HarperCollins Publishers, 1955) 325–26.

Chapter 4

A Question about Relationships

"If you love those who love you, what reward do you have?" (Matthew 5:46)

Many people are disturbed by the idea of rewards within religion. Some say rewards demean true religion: "If rewards are what you seek," they say, "then you're only in it for what you can get out of it." Others object to dangling rewards before people, believing it's a crass means of appealing to pie-in-the-sky promises rather than working for here-and-now results.

I truly appreciate the concerns within both objections. But I find it difficult to rewrite the Bible to conform to these high-minded protests. The awkward truth is that the Bible is chock-full of promised rewards (although many are significantly more nuanced in their statement than casual readers realize). So, as much as I can resonate with the objections, I can't endorse them. It's impossible for me to delete, dismiss, or dilute the multitude of promised rewards that fill the Bible's pages.

Fortunately, in this particular question of Jesus, the reward he mentions doesn't pose a problem. For that matter, neither here nor anywhere else in the Gospels does Jesus promise an ocean-view condo in the New Jerusalem or a six-course dinner with the Virgin Mary as a reward. In this particular instance, Jesus doesn't even drag God into the picture or offer any heavenly reward. His question is about human behavior and the mutual back scratching that's typical of everyday relationships. "If you love those who love you, what reward do you have?"

Jesus isn't dealing with celestial matters here, but with a very terrestrial matter—how we treat one another. There's nothing new in the fact that the "L" word shows up in this question; Jesus spoke about Love a great deal. Nor is there any real news in the fact that love is one of the greasiest words in our present-day vocabulary. You can over-hear folks talking about how much they "love" everything from peanut butter to Netflix to the Green Bay Packers. I'm confident they mean that they really, really like these things, that they have a heartfelt affection for them. However, this kind of "love" isn't what Jesus meant. My forays into the dense forests of New Testament scholarship assure me that the word "love" as Jesus used and meant it translates into respectful, open, honest dealings with others. The opposite, I guess, would be disrespectful, inconsiderate, indifferent, and perhaps even shady dealings. That's how you'd be expected to treat unloved folks.

What Jesus observed was the frequency with which others were treated "lovingly" only after they'd shown they deserved that kind of favorable treatment. That is, only after they had "loved" you. Thus his question, "If you deal respectfully and considerately with others only after they treat you that way, what reward do you have?"

One plausible answer to his question might be, "Well, I'll have some reliable, mutually supportive connections. I'll know whom to trust, and be spared a lot of disappointment and headaches—and that's no small reward."

True enough. But there's also a down side. Shouldn't we note, for example, that this procedure reduces us to being just *responders?* Our behavior is no longer self-originating; it's dependent on others' behavior. We lose our autonomy and therefore a bit of our selfhood when we let our treatment of others be determined by their treatment of us. Sadly, there's a kind of voluntary slavery visible here—and it's always sad when anyone created to stand tall and proud in God's own image is reduced to servility to another human. In effect, then, the reward Jesus foresees in his question is more like a curse than a reward!

Jesus' alternative is for us to retain our freedom and not be manip-ulated by others' actions. At its heart, Jesus' alternative is a call to practice indiscriminate good toward all people, regardless of their actions. His way is to be initiators, people who launch relationships with fairness and trust. Without being needlessly stupid, such people love from the get-go, lead with the heart, and, yes, inevitably risk disappointment and loss and open themselves to the derision of the shrewd.

I'm not naïve enough to miss the fact that there are sharks in the sea, nor am I unrealistic enough to say it's easy to swim among them. I've learned that there are indeed long-toothed sharks, even in the nicest of waters, and sometimes they attack without any known provocation. But if you live only with an eye for sharks, you miss the beauty of the sea. Your reward is a keen eye for sharks but a blind eye to everything else. In time you could even begin to see a shark lurking behind every little guppy. What kind of reward is that?

I once heard it said of a certain high-profile church executive that he didn't have friends so much as he had allies. It was amazing to witness how shrewdly the fellow accrued allies, "loving" those who could and would "love" him back. He was a master at it. But sadly, when the time came for them to "love" him back, his allies melted like butter. He soon fell from view, unmourned. Quite a reward.

In another place in the Gospels, Jesus talks about the same issue in a somewhat different manner. He points to those whose names show up most often on the invitation lists for our dinner parties. As a general rule, they are people who have the means to invite us to their dinner parties. Consequently, our relational circle can become a tight-knit club of the well heeled and reciprocally obligated.

I'm confident that Jesus had no intention of putting the kibosh on dinner parties where good friends enjoy one another's company. After all, he seems to have enjoyed such occasions himself—like at the home of Martha and Mary and their brother Lazarus. What I think bothered him was our tendency to close ranks and deal only with those who are just like us, to scratch the backs only of some. The Jesus way is to scratch the backs of those who may not even have the arms, let alone the strength to scratch us back. Take the initiative! Expand the invitation list! Invite someone who has no dining room! Become an indiscriminate doer of good—like God—

without calculating the probability of getting your evening's meal and entertainment back. Even if it backfires, do it.

I had this pounded into me once as I returned from lunch to the church I was serving at the time. As I stepped from my car, a stranger walked across the parking lot toward me, introduced himself, and told me that on several previous occasions he'd sent his hourly employees to our church's clothing ministry to receive free work clothes. Unfortunately, he himself was now in dire straits and wanted to know if I could give him $213, which would pay his motel bill so that he and his sick wife could keep the room they'd occupied for a week. I told him our church didn't usually hand out cash to anyone, and certainly never in that amount, and that my colleague who handled these requests was out that afternoon. But I promised to call his motel and attempt to get an extension of time until my colleague could assist him. I also gave him all the cash I had on me—$12—and wrote down his cell phone number so I could call him later that afternoon about my contact with the motel office.

When I got to my office at church, I called the motel but wasn't able to get past the automated answering machine, and so I turned to the work on my desk. Sadly, I forgot to retry the call. At three o'clock, my secretary interrupted me to say Mr. So and So had called to ask if I had any money or a motel time extension to report. My conscience was stricken. I told her to call him and ask him to come back by the church in thirty minutes. I hustled to a nearby bank, withdrew $200 from my checking account, placed the bills in an envelope, and asked my assistant to give it to him when he arrived. All this on a Friday afternoon.

At 8:30 the next morning, I received a phone call at my home from this man. Surprised that he'd taken the initiative to find my home phone number, I assumed that he was calling to express thanks for the money. After all, I'm not in the habit of handing out $200 donations to strangers and felt pretty proud of myself for my generosity. But rather than giving me a cozy moment to feel virtuous about the greatness of my kind heart, what I heard was this: "Hey, I guess I didn't make myself clear; I needed $213, not $200! So, since I couldn't pay the full amount, the motel kicked my sick wife and me out last night, and I spent the money on some other things we needed. So I'm back to square one and still don't have a place to spend the night. Can you help me?"

I mumbled something about $212 being as far as I could go, and hung up—inwardly raging about this ingrate's unforgivable pushiness. My dismay continued to smolder all day Saturday and right up into the middle of my Sunday morning pastoral prayer. But then, in front of God and everybody listening to my finely intoned pieties, I realized that the guy had actually treated me much like I often treat God, over-looking the generosity and griping about the gap. As I stumbled to my prayer's Amen, my chastened soul was asking, "Well, Bozo, if you felt used by one brazen hustler, what kind of disappointment do you suppose has coursed through heaven from the abuse of all humankind across the centuries?"

One of the grandest images of God in the Bible is of One who gives to all without consideration of worthiness, without calculating the probability of appreciation or of return. Such generosity stands in shaming contrast to my $212—and invites me to do better.

Consider the story of Larry Stewart, a resident of Kansas City, Missouri, whose early adult days were spent in bad-luck poverty. On a bitterly cold day in 1979, he had the unusual good luck to have a little spare cash in his pocket, and he gave a generous tip to a carhop who was shivering in a flimsy coat. Her eyes filled with tears as she told him he had no idea what that tip meant to her. He was deeply moved by her gratitude, and a few years later, when he became a wealthy man, he began a practice of driving around Kansas City look-ing for people who seemed like they needed help. In the early years, he carried five- and twenty-dollar bills to give away, but eventually he worked his way up to one-hundred-dollar bills. When I heard about Larry Stewart, he estimated he'd distributed upwards of a million dollars in his random giveaway work.

When a newspaper reporter tracked him down to ask about his odd philanthropy, Stewart gave a good bit of credit to that exchange with the carhop as the genesis of his generosity. But his unique way of giving, he said, actually came from another encounter during the days when he was still walking the streets of Kansas City, homeless.

Desperately broke and having not eaten in two days, he went into a diner, ordered a full breakfast, and wolfed it down. When it came time to pay the bill, he told the waitress he'd lost his wallet. Overhearing the heated conversation between Stewart and the exasperated waitress, the owner of the diner came over to Stewart, looked him in the eye, and, slipping a twenty-dollar bill into Stewart's hand, quietly said, "You must have dropped this."[1]

One of the reasons I can't dismiss the Bible's many reward statements is because I'm irrationally sure that somewhere, on some Hero's List of the All-time Good Guys, that diner owner's name is up in lights. This protector of a "bum's" dignity is being rewarded, if for no other reason than that he had no cause to expect any reward for doing the "loving" thing.

Okay, so what if his reward isn't an extra star in his heavenly crown or the regular appearance of his name streaming on a celestial marquee? Maybe his reward is simply Larry Stewart's subsequent million-dollar giveaway. If so, I suspect that diner owner is well pleased with the astonishing proceeds from a twenty-dollar investment.

I'd like to hush now, since I've said all I know to say in response to this question of Jesus. But I can't get out the back door because there's still an awkward dilemma sitting here on the front porch. The question I've been considering is, unfortunately, at the tail end of Jesus' larger question of how we are to treat those who actually do us harm. Here's the full quote from Matthew 5:43-46a: "You have heard that it was said, 'You shall love your neighbors and hate your enemies.' But I say to you, Love your enemies and pray for those who persecute you so that you may be children of your Father in heaven; for he makes his sun rise on the evil and on the good, and sends rain on the righteous and on the unrighteous. For if you love those who love you, what reward do you have?"

It's one thing to love those who have been neutral toward us, who haven't particularly "loved us" but who haven't abused us, either. It's quite another to love those who have done us injury. How can anyone speak of considerate generosity of spirit when great sums of money have been lost or deep bonds of trust have been betrayed—or in times of international conflict? To speak of loving those who've done you harm in such times is to appear idiotic in the first two instances and unpatriotic or gutless in the third.

I've heard it said that we live in a nastier world than Jesus ever knew and that this ever-increasing meanness justifies us, if not requires us, to answer with force rather than with Jesus' "love." When I consider this objection, though, I can't see much evidence that the Roman Empire was very genteel. The days when Jesus walked this earth were "crude and cruel days and human life was cheap," according to all accounts I've read.[2] When Jesus dealt with those who engineered his death, he didn't use sweet words—he called them "hypocrites" and graphically described their wickedness (see Matthew's scalding twenty-third chapter)—but neither did he call for retaliation or getting even with them. And, as the spiritual says, "he never said a mumblin' word" of condemnation to the Roman soldiers who humiliated, whipped, and crucified him. Apparently, the instigators as well as the perpetrators of his death were included within his final "they know not what they do" petition for forgiveness. That way of relating to enemies was astonishing two thousand years ago, and its absurdity hasn't lessened since then. Though he has many believers, in this way of behaving Jesus has few followers.

I don't pretend to know what his outrageous commandment or his blood-red example means for every conflict of history or those crushing occasions when great injury has been done to me or those I love. But I can't escape their standing indictment of the futility of force and their reminder of the self-reduction that is our "reward" when we let the behavior of others dictate our own.

Once again, the Stranger who knows how to ask questions pushes us to the wall—and waits for a worthy answer.

Jesus, you know much better than I that loving one's enemies is hard work. It couldn't have been easy for you to live as you did—considerately, even among the viciously religious—or to die as you did—forsaken by those you'd loved. Loving others is hard work. It's your kind of work. My hope rests on the proposition that you'll never quit it, not least of all because I am as much in need of

*that love as anyone. Help me learn to love as you did and do—
not with sloppy, silly indulgence but with openhearted, tough
goodwill to all regardless of what they've earned or deserve. Amen.*

NOTES

1. Leonard Pitts, Jr., "Ailing Santa's Credo: 'Tis Better to Give,'" *The
Oklahoman*, 27 November 2006, 12A.

2. G. A. Studdert-Kennedy, "Indifference," *Sorrows of God and Other Poems*
(London: Hodder and Stoughton, 1921) 34.

Chapter 5

A Question about Faith

*"When the Son of Man comes, will he find faith
on earth?" (Luke 18:7)*

"Son of Man" is a complex term in the Bible. You could go semi-insane
trying to track the countless nuances scholars have found within it.
But among the consensus opinions is the conclusion that "Son of
Man" was not code language for Jesus' humanity. That is, it's not an
indicator that he was really a flesh-and-blood person, any more than
"Son of God" is code-language for his deity. Of course, Christian
orthodoxy insists that Jesus was indeed a real flesh-and-blood person
just like you and me, but that conviction is based on considerations
other than the term "Son of Man."

Instead, scholars believe this term is something like a nickname
Jesus gave himself, a name he took from Old Testament passages that
talk about a mysterious Son of Man appearing at the end of all things.
And that leads us precisely to the way Jesus uses this nickname in this
saying. He talks about "when the Son of Man *comes*," a fairly obvious
reference to what we today call the Second Coming of Christ. So the
question can be rephrased like this: "When I, the world-ender, return
in victory, will I find faith on earth?"

Not to be flippant about it, but this sounds like a question Jesus
must have asked after a terrible, horrible, no-good, very bad day (with
apologies to Judith Viorst). If you listen to the words spoken here,
what you hear is the voice of the man Christians deem to be God-
in-flesh actually wondering out loud if faith is going to make it on
this wacky planet! It's certainly not the kind of line the Positive
Thinker's edition of the Bible would highlight in color as an encour-
aging word for the downcast. "Jesus worries about the future" isn't a
line you'd want appearing at the top of a Bible page.

Perhaps Jesus wasn't reaching for a white towel of defeat when he spoke this question. Maybe his question strikes me this way only because my own confidence sometimes tanks, and so I like to find (create?) evidence that Jesus was also subject to such fluctuations in faith. So interpreting this question my way gets me off the hook for being such an up-and-down believer—and it supplies me with wonderful ammo to fire back at my more exuberant believer friends who worry about me because I'm not as jubilant as they are.

Nonetheless, even if I'm guilty of reading my own issues into this question, it wouldn't be the first time someone misconstrued a text because his or her own baggage kept them from interpreting it more accurately. Scholars acknowledge this and even have terms and explanations for how it happens.

For instance, such lopsided understanding is often said to be the result of the interpreter's *pre-condition* or the interpreter's *social location.* Both terms essentially mean you can't jump out of your own skin. Pre-condition and social location explain why, for centuries, the principal interpreters of Scripture—for the most part, white males with academic backgrounds—saw meanings that reinforced the white, male status quo in biblical texts. But when "others" (women, the poor, people of color) began to bring their social locations and pre-conditions to the same texts, the results were astounding. Old stories took on new meanings, and cherished truths were turned upside down. This is why we see so many fresh interpretations of the Bible offered today. All kinds of folks have discovered that this is a sacred game any number can play.

When the number and diversity of biblical interpreters grow, so does our response to Jesus' question about the future of faith on earth. If we each bring our cultural, emotional, sexual, and theological perspective to the adventure of life and the documents of faith, can we reasonably imagine that each will come away believing the same as her neighbor? Our vantage determines our vision. Remember the lighthearted old piece about the Six Wise Men of Hindustan?

> There were six men of Hindustan, to learning much inclined,
> Who went to see an elephant, though all of them were blind,
> That each by observation might satisfy his mind.

The first approached the elephant, and happening to fall
Against his broad and sturdy side, at once began to bawl,
"This mystery of an elephant is very like a wall."

The second, feeling of the tusk, cried, "Ho, what have we here,
So very round and smooth and sharp? To me 'tis mighty clear,
This wonder of an elephant is very like a spear."

The third approached the elephant, and happening to take
The squirming trunk within his hands, thus boldly up and spake,
"I see," quoth he, "the elephant is very like a snake."

The fourth reached out an eager hand, and felt above the knee,
"What this most wondrous beast is like is very plain" said he,
"'Tis clear enough the elephant is very like a tree."

The fifth who chanced to touch the ear said, "E'en the blindest
    man
Can tell what this resembles most; deny the fact who can;
This marvel of an elephant is very like a fan."

The sixth no sooner had begun about the beast to grope,
Than seizing on the swinging tail that fell within his scope;
"I see," said he, "the elephant is very like a rope."

So six blind men of Hindustan disputed loud and long,
Each in his own opinion exceeding stiff and strong;
Though each was partly in the right, they all were in the wrong![1]

It is important to remember that people approach faith from
many different routes. Some come from homes where abuse or hunger
was the norm; they may find God's existence, let alone God's good-
ness, hardly credible. Some come from lives of privilege or
self-sufficient cynicism; they may find it difficult to give credence to
God's humility. Some people's personality is introspective, and they
find it impossible to find God's presence in an exuberant environ-
ment. Others are action-oriented people-persons and grow catatonic
in the cerebral reverence of some forms of High Church. Some are

left-brained, others are right-brained, and some make others wonder
if a brain was ever bestowed on them! The variations among us are
endless, and it is futile to imagine we are all going to come out of the
faith-search with the same vision, or the same passion and theological
stance. This very fact ought at least keep us from the arrogance overheard in a conversation between a Baptist and an Episcopalian in
which the Baptist played his meanest card last by saying, "Well, friend,
let's just agree that you will worship the Lord in your way and I will
worship Him in His."

Tennyson more helpfully captured faith's proper humility in his
famous lines:

> Our little systems have their day,
> They have their day and cease to be
> They are but broken lights of thee
> And thou, O Lord, art more than they.[2]

But what, pray tell, does all this have to do with the actual substance
of the question, "But when the Son of Man comes, will he find faith
on earth?" Simply this: when Jesus uttered his question about the
future of faith, I don't think he was referring to the survival of worship
forms or doctrine or dogma. These issues, as significant as they may
be, don't appear to have been his concern at this moment. His interest
was primarily in the lived, experiential dimension of faith. And true
to form, the paragraph in which his faith question appears is one that
deals with the most essential dimension of faith: prayer.

What is a better litmus test for living faith than prayer? We may
engage in many other so-called religious acts for a variety of reasons,
but the only reason I can imagine anyone would pray is because they
believe—or *want* to believe. You might do good deeds with laudable
humanitarian motivations. You might attend church services for
aesthetic or social reasons. You might affirm creeds for conformist
reasons. You might even make large donations for tax or public
acclaim reasons. But, you pray because you believe Someone is listening and capable of response. At the least, you don't keep on
praying—and that is Jesus' concern in this question—if you don't

believe God is on the other end of the line, a willing participant in the conversation. Your time is too valuable to waste it on prayer if, as Huck Finn concluded, "it don't do no good."

So Jesus' question may be aimed at one momentous issue: Will the hopeful, trusting interaction with God that we call prayer persist until the end? Or will the acids of doubt and the mold of religiosity cause us to let prayer slide into the dustbin of abandoned practices?

Here is one of those times when we may be tempted to scurry off into the bushes and craft seven fashionable alternatives to old-fashioned prayer—anything actually—to escape a true assessment of the liveliness of believing, trustful prayer. Like skillful politicians who reframe an interviewer's direct question, we'd much prefer to reframe or sidestep this one altogether. After all, our images of ourselves as good-enough Christians takes a punch in the gut if we admit that prayer for us is more a subject for discussion than a holy habit, or confess that we actually negotiate life more with a nod toward God than with knees and spirit reverently bowed. To admit this would be an indicting admission that Jesus' question already has a disappointing answer.

We have our excuses. Somewhere near the top of the list for many of us is our puzzlement about how and if prayer "works." I'll own up to it; I often question whether it "works" at all, in the sense of extracting blessings from Above. If it does, there surely seems to be a capriciousness to it that defies understanding. On other days, better days, I entertain the thought that praying is less a matter of filing requests than of drawing near to the Infinite Center of all things. To pray is more like stilling myself in the presence of Mystery and letting my shopping list drop to the floor, content just to "be," and to be lost in gratitude. On still other days, I'm zealously lobbying for all manner of things, tossing aside my reservations about prayer as though I'd never heard of Isaac Newton or cause and effect and how the world *really* works. I am, in truth, all over the place when it comes to believing prayer—and that creates uneasiness within me.

One quick escape route, and it's one I've often traveled, is to blame my lack of praying not on prayer's intellectual puzzles but on the

disgusting distortions of it to be heard in countless venues. I've heard
public prayers that were as regrettable as this:

> Father God, I just want to praise and thank you for giving me a
> blessed life. And I just want to ask you, Father God, to keep me
> and my stuff safe and secure, maintaining a protecting hedge
> around me and my family from the enemy's attacks. Father God, I
> just want to ask you to guide me so that I might not sin against
> Amazon.com or be left behind when the after-Christmas sales
> begin. Amen.

Or this:

> Oh Thou, who art suffusing all mortal strivings with a transmogri-
> fying beneficence exceeding our Lilliputian cerebral powers, we
> would entreat thine approbation in all our exigencies and extrem-
> ities, now and henceforth, world without end. Amen."

Really?

As off-putting as such (admittedly over-the-top) prayers may be,
eventually I acknowledge that others' distortions don't legitimize my
neglect. I dare not use them as an excuse for not offering better,
worthier prayers carved from "out of the depths," offered day after
day until the Son of Man comes.

In fact, the paragraph in which Jesus' question is found concerns
prayer *in extremis*, with the "out of the depths" passionate prayers of
those who are dealing with injustice and deprivation. They have no
resource or recourse other than God, and therefore it is God's door
upon which they beat. Prayer in this context is not a device to enlarge
one's territory or obtain more bling. It's an audacious reliance on a
caring God for life's essentials (daily bread).

Jesus' model prayer endorses prayer that asks for things for
ourselves: "give us this day our daily bread." But when you think
about it, asking for daily bread is a pretty scary practice. To pray it
sincerely and literally would mean standing in a very different social
location than I have ever known. It would mean having no loaf of
bread already in the pantry and no automobile handy to run to the

store where three or thirty more loaves could be bought. To pray for "our daily bread" says we come to God as hand-to-mouth beggars, not as God's well-to-do neighbors.

Few of us, however, are likely to divest ourselves of our possessions so that we might be able to pray for "our daily bread" in this literal sense—at least that's certainly not an item on my to-do list. But perhaps what's on God's agenda is for us to display our professed faith (1) by generous giving in order that these hand-to-mouth beggars might actually have something to eat; (2) by relentless challenging of the entrenched policies that damn them to perpetual hunger; and (3) by actually praying for them. Praying God's special care for them is one evidence of an absurd yet enduring belief that God does still care about what happens on planet Earth—and has the power to make it whole.

I have a hunch that this is the kind of faith Jesus will be looking for "when the Son of Man comes." I hope he finds it.

Jesus, it's said that you got up early in the morning and found quiet places to pray—and that you were praying with your disciples at the Last Supper and in the Garden of Gethsemane and even on the Cross. You never quit, even when it seemed pointless to persist. I'm not like that. On some of my best days, and even my tough ones, praying is minimal. Your pattern shames me—and attracts me. Help me to want to pray. Above all, keep me from a faith that's satisfied to talk about you but seldom to you; grow in me a faith that walks and talks—even in prayer— like you. Amen.

NOTES

1. The version of the old story quoted here is from a poem titled "The Blind Men and the Elephant," written by John Godfrey Saxe in the nineteenth century.

2. From Alfred, Lord Tennyson, "In Memoriam A. H. H.," 1849.

Chapter 6

Questions about Authority

"What did Moses command you?" (Mark 10:3)
"What then does this text mean?" (Luke 20:17)

A worthy adage says, "Those who would sew must first tie a knot." Even those whose experience with a needle and thread is limited to an occasional button replacement have no trouble understanding this. Unless you want to re-stitch that button every week or so, an anchoring knot is essential.

But the adage isn't really about sewing, is it? It's about a major issue of life. Specifically, who or what are we going to accept as the anchoring "knot" for our lives? From seamstresses and tailors, who put our clothes together, we "butchers, bakers, and candlestick makers" are hereby given a first lesson about putting our life together: unless we want a lifetime of embarrassing do-overs and/or the humiliation of always being unbuttoned, we need a "knot": we need to have some kind of constant that gives us our bearings.

Initially our parents, our church, or our immediate culture told us where and what the knot was. We accepted their understanding of wrong and right, of what was important and what was negligible, what was sacred and what was not. This is where we began, trusting that what we were seeing or being told was the way it really was.

But at some point that confidence was shaken—at least that's the case for most of us. We learned that other people have tied their knots very differently and/or at different places. We perceived that our tribe's way of life wasn't the only way life can be understood and lived. Thus we were introduced to the question of authority. Whose voice or teaching—what philosophy or dogma or experience or feeling or book or tradition—are we building our lives on?

So much of life boils to down to daily decisions, to countless choices about everything from the clothes we're going to wear today to the choice to wear any clothes at all. Well, okay, the "clothing-optional" choice isn't a true choice, and I use it only as a ludicrous example. But it does illustrate the fact that at some point, our civilization chose to outlaw nudity. Why? Is it written somewhere in the skies that the human body must be covered? Who said so? And is that an authority we ought to pay attention to? These are the kinds of questions—frivolous and deadly serious—that are buried within the challenge of tying a knot.

For Jesus, this kind of question was framed in terms of ancient texts, the sacred scrolls that he as a faithful Jew believed were the "knot" God had given to his people, Israel. Thus, "What did Moses command?" was and is a baseline question for any observant Jew. They believed that through the commandments of Moses one heard the definitive word of God. Presumably you can't go any farther up the chain of command than that!

For many people today, however, it's not so obvious that Moses' words—or any other ancient religious texts, for that matter—say anything applicable to us. It is bizarre, admittedly, that supposedly intelligent twenty-first-century people would imagine that words written on parchment by people living in tents and mud houses with no electricity three thousand years ago might have anything relevant, let alone authoritative, to say to us. Those who do entertain the belief that Moses' words are still worthy of consideration are quick to add that Moses did not speak on his own. He spoke for God, and thus his words bear a greater signature than that of a fellow mortal. To those who shake their heads in wonderment about this claim, I can reply only that Jesus clearly believed this and that he was not the last to do so. For him, "What did Moses command you?" was *the* knot-tying question *par excellence.*

But for him there was more to it than simply knowing your Moses. Jesus asks not just what Moses commanded. He adds a most important companion question: "What then does this text mean?" To be sure, he didn't pose these two questions in the same conversation, but, as I trust this chapter will demonstrate, his consistent approach to the commandments makes it clear that he believes both quotation and interpretation are essential. In other words, it is one thing to quote a commandment. It is another thing to say what that commandment means. Even if you can quote your Moses chapter and verse, you still have to do your homework and ask what in the world—that is, in your present world—that ancient instruction means for today.

It's helpful to see how Jesus himself practiced this double discipline of quotation and interpretation. For example, there are times when he quoted a biblical text as being the final and irrevocable word on a matter, anchoring himself in the words of the book as though they were eternal bedrock. An example is found in his temptation experience recorded in Matthew 4 and Luke 4. In this event, Jesus repeatedly and stoutly rejects the tempter's every suggestion by quoting commandments from Moses. He "throws the book" at the tempter as though the book's words were an invincible sword placed in Jesus' hand by no less than God. But on other occasions, such as when he and his disciples grew hungry on a Sabbath, he had no qualms about disregarding another Mosaic commandment that prohibits "harvesting" on the Sabbath. When his hungry entourage boldly plucked some grain and ate it on the Sabbath, his critics protested that he was breaking a commandment. Jesus didn't deny it—but he defended this "harvesting" by citing other Scripture. (See Matthew 12:1-8.)

These passages tell me that sometimes Jesus interpreted the words of a text as being directly relevant, and therefore he was content to tie his knot there. But in other circumstances the words of one text had to be placed in conversation with other texts in order to discern God's will. Some were stand-alone commandments, while others had to be weighed in light of other statements in other passages. Interpretation was as important as quotation.

A still more radical variant of the way Jesus worked with Scripture is found in his Sermon on the Mount (Matthew 5–7). Early in the sermon he assures his audience that his intent is not to abolish or break, and certainly not to teach others to break, the commandments of Moses and the later prophets (5:17ff). He even scolds those who would do so. But then he immediately cites six different commands of the Old Testament ("You have heard that it was said . . .") and in each case counters the current understanding of that command with his own contrasting view ("But I say unto you . . ."). Every time, he offers a radical interpretation that expands the prevailing, more literal understandings of those texts.

Consider yet another example of his approach to Scripture. For centuries, the Jews had observed a distinction between clean and unclean foods; Moses himself is credited as being God's conduit for the rules concerning kosher foods (see Leviticus 11). A disregard for these dietary laws was a primary reason for the famous Maccabean revolt against Rome—wars were waged over this identity marker! Nonetheless, Jesus dared to say, "It is not what goes into the mouth that defiles a person, but it is what comes out of the mouth that defiles" (Matt 15:11). Thus, with one sentence, Jesus set aside the entire structure of clean and unclean foods and declared an entire chapter of his people's Bible as invalid. No wonder his disciples quickly asked him, "Do you know the Pharisees took offense [read, "were deeply offended"] when they heard what you said?"

At the very least, Jesus was no slavish literalist when it came to sacred texts. He felt free to work with the revered texts and to offer his own (re)interpretation of their meaning—if not to set them aside completely. For him there was the commandment and there was the interpretation of the commandment—these two—and they were equally important.

I think it's important now to add that Jesus wasn't the only one who engaged in this kind of "yes and no" approach to sacred texts. It's one thing to note that he, being the Son of God, worked with the texts rather than always bowing to them in their inherited form. But it's quite another to deduce from his precedent an inferred authorization for you or me to do the same. (Sorry, as nice as you may be, you don't yet qualify to be Jesus!)

The Old Testament book of Deuteronomy gives us evidence of ordinary humans doing just as Jesus did, that is, working reverentially and thoughtfully with inherited texts. Deuteronomy is one of the Old Testament's anchoring documents. It contains something close to a summary of what the Jews claimed as the unique word of God spoken to them through Moses. However, those who've spent decades studying countless ancient manuscripts say that Deuteronomy gives abundant evidence that the original Moses tradition—that is, the actual dictates of the historical character Moses—were amended by scribes multiple times. In each instance, the alteration came in response to new challenges not known to the Israelites of Moses' day. For instance, our present book of Deuteronomy contains rules for handling social and domestic dilemmas of *urban* life, even though during Moses' lifetime Israel was still a nomadic people without any land or cities. Examples of this are its guidance for such urban matters as awarding compensation to those injured by falling roof tiles, and even a process for selecting a new king—a political arrangement Moses' theocratic passions would have considered anathema. Linguistic scholars add to the evidence by noting that Deuteronomy includes words and terms that didn't appear in Israel's vocabulary until centuries after Moses' time. My conclusion is that long before Jesus ever laid eyes on the words of Moses, humans had worked with Moses' teachings and had offered interpretive restatements and additions.

The same kind of re-traditioning is found in Isaiah 56, which revises if not actually overrules statements in Deuteronomy 23:1-3. Most breathtaking of all, however, is the example of Jesus' own followers who set aside the fourth of the Ten Commandments ("Remember the sabbath day, and keep it holy") in favor of Sunday as their day of worship, and also set aside the Scripture-based practice of circumcision as a condition for inclusion within God's covenant people (see Acts 15). In neither of these cases is there any record of a voice from above authorizing them to take such action. Closer to our own times, Christians universally denounced the practice of human slavery as evil, even though the Bible never does so. Christians of long ago and of much nearer times have demonstrably looked at their existing context and circumstances and made the choice to disagree with or to reinterpret the meaning of the letter of sacred texts.

So it won't do to contend that Jesus alone had the privilege of respectfully offering interpretations or restatements of words appearing on a sacred page. Jesus stood in a noble lineage of predecessors who worked with authoritative texts, and he also spawned followers who did the same—always seeking to express the present shape of faithfulness to God, mindful of—but not bound to—past precedent.

In light of this, I find myself puzzled by those who imagine they can settle all matters for all time and all situations simply by quoting a verse from the Bible. The Bible itself reveals that it's just not that simple. Jesus didn't let his contemporaries get by with simply spouting verses from the holy book. He pushed them—by means of his own dealings with texts and by questions like "What does this text mean?"—to understand that healthy, helpful knot-tying requires painstaking interpretation as well as quotation.

In other words, questions of authority have never been a walk in the park, not even for the people we read about within the Bible. They, like we, wrestled with ancient words and present dilemmas. They, like we, had to decide their way forward. Sometimes they honored the ancient words at face value, while at other times they honored them with a fresh interpretation. But they tied their knots with materials drawn from within the working of God in their lives and community; they tied their knots with materials drawn from the book; they *worked with* these texts. They didn't just pitch out the old as outdated nonsense and cobble up new, jazzier guidebooks to suit the whimsy of the moment. Within a context of reverence, they sought the relevance of what Moses and his successors had left for their guidance.

If we are wise, we still do. That doesn't mean it's become simpler. I have a friend who is gay; he's also someone who has read the Bible and actually knows what's in it. His question to me is why we give so much continuing authority to Moses' words about homosexuality but consider Moses' commandment to stone a disobedient child as obviously irrelevant, if not unthinkably repugnant. The two commandments come from the same Mosaic tradition, he says, so why are gays stigmatized while the kid who is a holy terror is allowed to live, scream, and bully his way through life? Good question.

Rachel Held Evans, a thirty-ish evangelical blogger/author, has written a book titled *A Year of Biblical Womanhood* recounting her yearlong experiment in obeying as literally as possible every biblical command about and for women. Her report is simultaneously hilarious, educational, painful, and thoughtful. If nothing else, her *Year* illustrates how impossible it is to understand, let alone practice, every supposed divine commandment saddled upon women.

These are just two examples of how devilishly difficult it is to master the art of knot tying. History is replete with similar stories. One of my favorites harks back to the infamous British king, Henry VIII, who considered himself a student of Scripture. Thus when his need to produce a male heir for the English throne made it urgent for him to shed his wife, Catherine—who had borne him no male child—he found a Bible verse to support his divorce intentions. Catherine had previously been the wife of Henry's brother Arthur, and only by means of a papal dispensation had she been permitted, upon Arthur's death, to marry Henry. However, since she bore Henry no male heir, he found a verse from the Bible that gave him an authority higher than the Pope's. Leviticus 20:21 said, "And if a man shall take his brother's wife, it is an unclean thing; he hath uncovered his brother's nakedness; they shall be childless." Henry concluded that, regardless of the papal dispensation, he and Catherine were under a divine curse; Catherine had to go—and go she did! (Along with several others, as we know.)

Such shenanigans of blessing one's desires with a text lead me to believe that second only to the risk God took by creating humans is the risk God took by going into print. That set the stage for our tragic and often blood-soaked history of battles over words we believe to be straight from God. (But in all those battles for God, does God not usually become the sorrowing, forgotten figure on the sideline?)

Ostensibly God knew all this from the get-go, but nonetheless thought it was worth the gamble. Surely God could have come up with some other, non-textual way of informing successive generations of the God-story, but providing written minutes of the previous meetings seems to be the method God chose. Jesus' questions, then, are still the pertinent ones: "What does the book say?" and "What do the book's statements mean?"

There have been times when I've wanted to turn these questions back on Jesus and ask, "If you were here today and could see the global religious mess we are in, how would you interpret these texts?" For instance, when religiously fed animosity, if not violence, has become a daily fact, how might he interpret "No one comes to the Father but by me" (John 14:6)? Is it possible he might take that one back, or ask for a do-over, or offer a scintillating interpretation none of us dullards has ever dreamt? Or would he stand by it, and challenge us to "Deal with it!" Unfortunately, since we can't interview him, we must hazard our own answers as to what that blunt statement and all the other statements of Scripture mean.

My own beginning point for knot tying can be simply stated: you must know more than the words of the Bible to know God's word. That's not to say that the two are totally separate realities; it is to say that they aren't always identical. Just like the people in the Bible, I have to work with the various statements I read within the Bible. I dare not isolate just one sentence as being "the word of God"; I must read each sentence within the context of its surrounding sentences and its literary genre and its particular document. I must introduce it to other sentences about the same subject found in other portions of the Bible and listen to the ensuing conversation. I have to ask about the circumstances in which they were written and what each sentence was meant to say originally, and to whom. This of course means I must learn at least a smidgeon about the history and culture of those days. Only this kind of historical investigation gives me a window not only into what the text says but also what it originally meant.

Even with this historical/textual work, I'm still not assured I've come up with an acceptable answer as to what it might mean for today. John Wesley, the founder of Methodism, agreed that our search ought to begin by listening to the Bible. But then he went on to identify three other important sources for understanding. Those three are tradition, reason, and experience.

I'm not a Methodist or a Wesley scholar, so I can't say that my interpretation of these three would satisfy him, but here's my own understanding of them. By tradition, I mean I need to listen to what others seekers before my time have said about both the texts and the issue at hand. Tradition challenges me to learn not only from my biblical ancestors but also from my post-biblical ancestors. By reason,

I mean I need to compare my interpretation with the world of knowledge that's at my fingertips. If someone proposes an answer that seems wrong when put alongside what I find in widely respected biology or history or economics textbooks—that is, if someone pro- poses something that's sounds loopy in light of what we know otherwise—then I need to be leery. This doesn't mean I jettison every- thing that doesn't conform to society's prevailing politically correct gauge; it does mean I use my God-given intellectual abilities rather than park them when I'm engaged in this kind of knot tying. Finally, by experience I mean that my interpretations ought to ring true in my experience or the experience(s) of those I know of; those interpre- tations ought not to strike me as being completely foreign to the human experience.

Bottom line? Discerning the word of God requires serious mental engagement, not just the compilation of citations. And it requires even more than the intellectual work I've suggested here. Just as essen- tial, if not more so, is sincere "soul" work—the use of imagination, attentiveness, patience, humility, and yearning. This is a spiritual mat- ter, not just an academic game or philosophical pastime. After all, I'm seeking something much more important than a good hotel rate in Ottumwa, Iowa. I am seeking to discern the word and will of no less than God. I'm trying to tie a knot that will hold, even when most everything else is coming undone.

Now, a final essential. Absolutely essential in all of my seeking is collaboration with other seekers. As a matter of historical record, all the examples of "working with" texts noted in this chapter—except those attributed to Jesus—were the product of a community, not the personal opinion of one person. The surest route to error in every age is to work with these texts in isolation from others. I need the com- munity, the disciple band, the church as a circle of fellow interpreters. Their wisdom and counsel can spare me from quirky personal tan- gents. This is one more reason that if we didn't have the church we'd need to invent one; we need "a choir of questioners," a community to help us discern the path of wisdom. Otherwise one of Israel's sad descriptors becomes true of us: "all the people did what was right in their own eyes" (Judg 21:25).

This does not, however, mean that the individual's right and responsibility of interpretation are meaningless. We'd not have Protestantism today without the lonely voice of Martin Luther as he protested the majority reading of Scripture in 1517. But it's also necessary to remember that Luther was operating within a "community"—the writings of then-neglected authors like Augustine and others—and that his new readings of Scripture soon found the supportive "community" of others who were asking the same questions as Luther. There is a place therefore for both individual and corporate interpretation, but those of us who are less than Luther will do well to work elbow to elbow with others as we try to interpret Scripture.

So it comes down to this—at least for me. I do my homework and then I bet my life. Though I take counsel from as many sources as I may, eventually it's my choice, a daring decision to anchor my life here, or there, or somewhere else. Sometimes, but not always, that means I rest my weight on the printed word. On other days that means my knot isn't tied so much around any particular chapter or verse as it is around the character of God that I discern in the always astonishing character of Jesus of Nazareth. He becomes my court of last appeal. Do I make mistakes and sometimes opt for errors? Absolutely.[1] That's human. Regrettable, but human. Then, if never before, I tie my knot around the Jesus-painted portrait of the God of unfathomable grace.

I realize not everybody is as hung up on Jesus as I am. Not everybody is as concerned about what Moses said as I am. For that matter, I also realize that not everybody is convinced about the need to tie their knots with reference to God. I get that, and I want to respect every person's own way of processing their ethical decisions. But what I don't get and what I do have trouble respecting is anyone completely ignoring the question of knot tying and its importance. Sorry, but I'm too stunned by the world's beauty and too wary of the world's volatility to be patient with anyone who's not trying to act wisely, compassionately, and peacefully in a time when civilization dances on the edge of self-destruction.

Some have concluded that because religion has been at the heart of so much of the world's agonies, it ought to be banished from our society as a crime against humanity. Book-based believers particularly, it is said, have been among society's greatest enemies, invariably being belligerent bigots and narrow-minded fomenters of division. The charge stings because it has some unwanted truth within it—even if it sadly ignores the good we've also done. I hope, however, that the preceding paragraphs, while conceding the critic's point, have also suggested a way for people to continue opening themselves to the Bible as a guide for wise knot tying. I cannot believe the world will be bettered by dismissing the Bible's story and teachings. Rather, what Moses commanded and how Jesus and his followers worked with his words contain the hope this world needs. The Bible, interpreted wisely and lived creatively, provides the materials for sewing together a blessed life—and a durable world.

Jesus, between those who idolize the Bible as though it were God and those who dismiss it as though it were a fairy tale, it's difficult to come to a balanced view of the authority of the Bible. I really don't want to live on the skimpy rations of either left or right. So keep me open and learning, please. Be my teacher and help me to recognize the ring of truth, God's truth, wherever I hear it. And when I do hear it, give me the courage to live in its light for the good of my neighbor and to the glory of your name. Amen.

NOTE

1. Honesty demands that I also admit there are too many times when my decisions are made without regard for any of this. Having more than an inkling of what God's will is, I still choose to do it my way. I am an active sinner even on my saintliest days. Just like everyone else.

Chapter 7

A Question about Fear

"Why are you afraid? Have you still no faith?"
(Mark 4:40)

A newspaper cartoon depicted two moviegoers emerging from a theater whose marquee advertised a "Monster Movie Marathon." One patron says to the other, "For some reason scary movies just don't seem so scary anymore." I understand. When you are living with as many real-life threats as we presently face, *scary* is just another word for *normal.*

In the 1960s our international context was represented by a make-believe clock that nuclear scientists and military gurus reset periodically to indicate how many minutes remained until an atomic holocaust. As disturbing as that image was, it was softened by our optimism that surely no nation would actually be suicidal enough to fire a first missile. Now I'm not so sure.

That ticking clock hardly seems adequate now to capture the multiple causes for alarm in our world. "Rogue nations" and extremist groups led by rabid ideologues possessing high-power, long-range arsenals have become our new normal. "Little" wars with genocides venting centuries-old animosities—waged by people who are impervious to third-party interventions—have become our new normal. Political stalemates while financial, social, educational, and climatological crises pile ever higher have become our new normal. Terrorism, both domestic and international, dominates the news. There is much we might fear.

These situations cry out for many responses. But on my short list of most-needed items, I'd write and underline the word *wisdom.* When just one well-intended but bungled sentence or gesture from those at the helm could have catastrophic consequences, the gift of wisdom is not just appealing; it is essential.

But before I climb too far out on that wisdom limb, I note that when Jesus confronted a time of great fear, he didn't speak of wisdom. With his disciples frozen in fear and screaming for his help—their boat was about to capsize in a stormy sea—Jesus asked about faith: "Why are you afraid? Have you still no faith?" Jesus' concern was about their faith—not their wisdom.

That seems odd. Several of those disciples were professional fishermen, grown men who were wise in navigation and in the ways of this sea and her foul moods. Wouldn't "Use your heads!" have been a more useful response from Jesus? Trotting faith onto the stage—when it surely would have made more sense to encourage them to stay cool and use their sea smarts—strikes me as pious talk that is barely a shade away from "answerizing."

But before I climb too far out on this criticizing limb, there's a dimension of this faith-wisdom linking that I need to remember. It would be wrongheaded to depict these two, faith and wisdom, as opposites. It's more fitting to think of them in terms of priority rather than polarity. Their relationship isn't a matter of either/or; it's more like the relationship of mother and child. Faith creates the space where wisdom can function. Faith has the capability to calm us enough to think straight, enabling us to use whatever wisdom we have.

Consider the case of the man who is well known for his wisdom, King Solomon. When young Solomon ascended to the throne of his father King David, he prayed a famous prayer (2 Chr 1:7ff). Confessing his smallness in the face of the immense task before him, he asked God for wisdom. God praised him for his choice—and also gave him the desired wisdom. Generally this story is heard as support for the idea that wisdom is the great necessity. But isn't the story also reminding us that wisdom has its origin in faith?

Solomon understood that though his father, David, could grant him the nation's throne, he could not grant him the wisdom to occupy it well. Wisdom wasn't a hereditary endowment. Only God could confer such wisdom and only God could sustain it within the new king. Thus, Solomon prayed. From the stance of faith, he sought and received wisdom. And his administration's record shows that Solomon ruled well as long as his reliance on God continued to be central to his life. He became a royal disappointment only when his faith was more vested in political alliances and palace machinations than in God.

Wisdom is a delicate plant. Planted and carefully nurtured in the soil of faith, it can blossom, and in its shade peace can flourish. In an extreme sense wisdom may be seen as parasitic. That is, it draws its life from faith, but in a more holistic sense these two are symbiotic, each needing and drawing upon the other for its livelihood.

Certain psalms provide a helpful image of this faith-wisdom connection. In these particular psalms, the writers give thanks to God for having saved them from various perils. While that certainly isn't uncommon, the particular language these psalms use is distinctive. "You gave me a wide place for my steps under me" (Ps 18:36; see also Pss 4:1; 40:2) is the way they speak of God's salvation. The "wide place" discovered by these psalmists when they called on God in faith gave them a place to stand against the panic when life closed in on them. Through faith, the suffocating claustrophobia of fear was held at bay and they could breathe and see more clearly and thus keep things in perspective. These psalms give us yet another indicator that faith is essential for the stability and the courage to act with whatever wisdom we already have, let alone the additionally needed wisdom for the crisis hour.

But before I crawl too far out on this faith limb, I must add that there is faith and then there is FAITH. There is the kind of faith that gives birth to stability and wisdom in the storm, the kind of faith that might be best called trust. And there is also another kind of faith that gives birth to little other than brittleness. Perhaps this latter kind of faith might be better understood as an adherence to a certain ideology rather than a warm trust in the greatness of God. The center of gravity for this spurious kind of faith is a cluster of ideas (usually a political/economic/religious mixture, either perceptibly conservative or liberal in nature), not a rooted trust in the lively Mystery of the triune God of Christian faith. Thus it is a faith that is lashed to certain propositions as much as (if not more than) to God. God is simply the claimed authorizer of these propositions. There is usually little humility in this kind of faith; certainty is its truer trademark, and our scary times have no doubt contributed to its growth. Fearful people fervently clasp one-answer solutions to the threatening complexity of our world.

This kind of faith has claimed the deep loyalty of many born-again, Bible-quoting churchgoers. But in my opinion it's not the kind of faith that enables us to enter a happier, less fearful future. It is faith in a social agenda, not faith in a God whose ways are inscrutable, who grants bold, fear-expelling wisdom, gutsiness, and graciousness. Whether coming from the left or the right, this ideological faith feeds on fear and nurtures a fear-based smallness. Rather than enlarging our world, it produces a damning narrowness.

Yes, that's a harsh judgment, but I'll stick by it even as I admit I can't explain why it's so or suggest how to fix it. I just know that there are some for whom Christian believing is a marvelous aid to an enlivening vision of life together, while in others the very same religion seems to foster constricting, "answerizing" substitutes for a fear-facing, wisdom-granting faith.

Consider the unlikely example of Abraham Lincoln, whom I consider to be a man whose wisdom in fearful times was deeply rooted in faith, even though he was far from being a poster child of professed religious belief. Though he occasionally made his way to a Christian worship service (typically sitting alone in an anteroom of the sanctuary of the New York Avenue Presbyterian church in Washington, DC), he left no record of spiritual experience and never joined a church. In comparison to the ubiquitous, syrupy religiosity that filled the political rhetoric of his day, Lincoln's speech was noticeably spartan. His papers and speeches, however, reveal a profound faith and trust in the Mystery and Mercy surrounding all humankind—even his avowed enemies. His was a faith apparently wrought in brooding silence and private counsel before a God too large to capture under any church's tent or within its books of doctrine. But successive generations of scholars agree that his wisdom was largely responsible for successfully guiding this nation through its greatest crisis.

As well intended as each age's markers for true piety may be, I think Jesus calls us to a believing that is more *searching* than affirming certain propositions or engaging in certain religious practices, however valid or helpful these may be. For Jesus' panicked disciples on the stormy sea, it was a matter of trust in the rescuing power of the One Jesus called Father. For us, I think the needed faith is a lively trust in the steadfast presence of God with us—indeed, the presence of God in and with the entire groaning creation!—guiding, judging, forgiving, and sustaining.

It is important to underline that such faith in God is not so much a momentary spasm of heightened credulity as it the result of a growing, cumulative bond. Jesus' question is, "Are you *still* without faith?" The word *still* suggests to me that there were earlier experiences that deserved to be remembered as a basis for calmness in this crisis. Apparently he thought that past experiences with him should have prepared the twelve for the present hour. A path of trust could and should have been discovered through the varied experiences they had been through together.

Consider an inadequate parallel. I was nuts about my wife when I married her— and I still am—but it's a different and a better quality of nuttiness now. There was much we didn't know about each other when we married; indeed there was much we didn't know about ourselves and much more about ourselves that life hadn't yet called forth. After you've played out most of the story of your life with another person and you still are best friends, distrust is absent.

So it is with God. Deep trust takes time. Event by event, you "test the ice" to see if it is solid, and it's to be hoped that you discover it is so. But the testing process is essential because in that process, just as much unlearning takes place as learning. We unlearn false assumptions and unworthy expectations of the Other and of the relational life. Those sobering letting-go and recalibrating experiences are painful. But they orient us to truth and keep us from future forays onto ice that won't support us. And as a result, we grow in our confidence in this Invisible Companion. We learn not to be so afraid.

The Bible frequently reports God or angels telling people, "Fear not" or "Be not afraid." I haven't personally done the math, but a good friend of mine assures me that, contrary to the idea that the Bible is filled with "thou shalt nots," the Bible's "fear nots" are much more numerous. Even if my friend's math is off, his theology is on target.

One common surprise many of us have as we actually start reading the Bible in its grand sweep is that the God being talked about is intent upon blessing, not scolding. At times it's almost as though what you're reading is the world's first damage-control campaign—God methodically debunking life-choking rumors and exposing the falsity of fear-driven concepts. Sure, there are times, particularly in the Old Testament, when God rattles Israel's cage and rightly scares the hell out of them. But even then the intent is to liberate Israel from the fear-filled cage in which she has imprisoned herself by her God-ignoring ways. The rattling of that cage is meant to awaken Israel to the One who stands by the open door and is able to lead them into the liberty of the children of God.

I don't think God's intention has changed. Some of the situations that alarm us must surely be God's way of rattling our cages, calling us to repentance. But in every situation, fear subsides when we respond affirmatively to the One who invites us to stand with God in open spaces or walk with God toward promised lands. Incident by incident, storm by storm, we find ourselves less fearful—but never fearless!—and able to use all we know to good advantage.

As I've pondered the situation of Jesus' disciples on that stormy sea, I've wondered what the disciples imagined he might do in response. Calming seas wasn't Jesus' previous specialty. This was his and their first and only "storm" scene. Did they expect him to give orders to the winds and waves? Whatever their hopes may have been, their spirits were in agreement with a gospel song that says, "I must tell Jesus . . . Jesus can help me, Jesus alone." And Jesus did. With a word he stilled the stormy sea.

Well, that's what happened that night, but the same can't be said in every subsequent case. Any idea that such would be the case died on a Friday afternoon outside Jerusalem's walls. Jesus himself, hung on a cross, crying out to a silent sky, "Why have you abandoned me?" is evidence enough that the wand of faith doesn't overcome all dangers. But even at Golgotha, faith declares that God was at work in saving ways, even if not in a way that saved Jesus himself from perishing.

Many times it still appears that Jesus is asleep in the back of the boat like he was on the night when the sea turned ugly. But something of a powerful location joke is at work here. The help we seek isn't on another planet or behind lock and key in some cloudy heaven; it's right here in the boat with us. The God of farthest galaxies is with us, so, even if the boat sinks, we go down in the best of company.

As a matter of sober fact, we all will go down someday. Death exempts none of us. No person, no nation, no civilization, no institution endures forever. Why then permit fear to rule? Faith says that in life and in death the Lord is near. Faith enables us to use every bit of our knowledge and wisdom to preserve the things we love—or to let go of them in trust and with gratitude. Such faith provides the platform from which wise and courageous action can be launched, even in scary times.

In the late 1930s, long before a young white Baptist preacher named Clarence Jordan became the founder of Georgia's Koinonia Farms, the translator of the wickedly on-target *Cotton Patch Gospel*, and the spiritual father of Habitat for Humanity, he lived and worked in the Haymarket Community of Louisville, Kentucky—the roughest, poorest slum area of that city. He did so as an act of Christian discipleship, a choice to be among "the least of these." One day the area was electrified by the news that a white man had raped a young black girl. Enraged blacks began to gather at the Negro Fellowship Center to plan their response. Jordan slipped into the meeting and watched and listened as a large black man, waving a length of steel pipe in his hand, bellowed, "The whites would kill a Negro for this! Well, I'm gonna go kill me a white man!"

The young Jordan knew he must do something. He walked wordlessly to the front of the room, toward the livid man and the table that stood beside him, every eye in the room following his movement. Then, into the room's tense silence, Jordan said, "If a white man must die for this, let it be me. Do it now." Then he bent over, lowering his head to the table's surface to receive the blow.

The angry black man was stunned; his shoulders sagged and he lowered the pipe, speechless before Jordan's words and act. The observing crowd murmured in disbelief. The fury of their rage had been matched by a courageous deed. They began to talk about a better, nonviolent way to redress the ugly crime—a way they followed to good effect.[1]

I can't imagine I'd have had the wisdom, and certainly not the courage, to do what Jordan did that day. He probably even surprised himself. But I'm confident that as he lowered his head to that table, he believed Jesus was with him. My confidence is based on the knowledge that countless times in his later life Jordan displayed a similar trust in that same presence—especially when it was angry white segregationists who were waving the deadly weapons. Through it all, Jordan's trust was in God.

When eventually he did die, his friends put his body in a plain pine box for burial. As it was being lowered into the ground, a little girl—her first name was Faith—was observing the solemn ritual. She was too young to fully understand what was happening, but in her naiveté, three-year-old Faith Fuller offered the perfect benediction for this wise and courageous man. In the silence of the moment, Faith began to sing, "Happy birthday to you. Happy birthday to you. Happy birthday, dear Clarence. Happy birthday to you." Indeed.

Jesus, some leaders play on our fears and manipulate our anxieties in order to gain and keep power. You weren't like that. You talked about being unafraid of anything or anyone less than God. And then you said God could be trusted like a good Father who wants us to live with each other as caring sisters and brothers. You even became a thorn-crowned Elder Brother for us and promised you'd never abandon us, never let us sink alone, uncared for. You really aren't like those others, are you? In a time of terror, that's almost too good to be true. Almost. Amen.

NOTE

1. Henlee H. Barnette, *Clarence Jordan: Turning Dreams into Deeds* (Macon GA: Smyth & Helwys, 1992) 6.

Chapter 8

A Question about Integrity

*"You are the salt of the earth, but if salt has lost its taste,
how can its saltiness be restored?" (Matthew 5:13)*

It's a commonplace phrase for us now: "salt of the earth." But when Jesus spoke this expression into familiarity, it was a stunning declaration.

Remember the ordinary persons to whom this was first addressed—twelve who'd only recently been drafted from the shops and shorelines of Galilee. Not a one of them had a résumé that would commend him for special status. They were more like the dust of the earth than its salt. Even the Greek text reveals the surprise of these twelve being so designated. It places a "you" at the first of the sentence and then repeats it within the verb: "You . . . of all persons—you!"

The surprise is there because of the next words: you are the *salt*. At the time, Israel's Scriptures—the Torah, the words of instruction from God—were known as the salt. That treasured text preserved the distinct ways of God's people and provided for Israel the tangy taste of eternity. And now Jesus would amend this by declaring that simple, unlearned mortals are also the preservers of a holy identity and a taste of a realm beyond?

There is more. Like an ascending, carefully crafted drama, Jesus speaks his final crowning surprise. You are the salt *of the earth*. If anyone had previously supposed this Nazarene preacher was just a regional flash-in-the-pan, here was a bone-rattling wake-up call. This man has more in view than just the people called Israel. He's talking about the whole earth! He is daring to fill the ears of his inner circle with some grandiose ideas about the hope of the whole earth residing in them.

Curiously, his words have never been heard as a once-upon-a-time pronouncement only to his inner circle of twelve or even to the eavesdropping crowd. Jesus' followers across two millennia have always felt that he is looking them in the eye, speaking these words directly to them: "You, yes, *you* are the salt of the earth!" I confess this declaration continues to "get in my face," like my mother used to do physically when she had something most important for me to hear. Here are potent words. But what on earth do they mean?

Begin with the accepted understanding, that is, that salt was associated with the written basis for Israel's identity and way of being, the Torah. Thus, one twist is that this salt is now being personalized; ordinary mortals are said to be living scriptures, if you will. Very human people, rather than just hallowed words on sacred pages, are being thrust into the spotlight by Jesus.

There's also the consideration that salt in Jesus' day was the most common preservative known. Refrigeration was millennia away; salting was the only way to hold putrefaction at bay. So in Jesus' words there is also a declaration concerning earth's preservation—the whole earth's health, its viability as a place of habitation, is being placed in the hands of common folk.

Perhaps the most overlooked aspect of this statement is that it is a declarative sentence. You *are* the salt of the earth. There is no "you will be" or "you must be" in this utterance. It is an astonishing present tense declaration of existing fact. Jesus isn't issuing orders; he's declaring what is. He's not giving them something to do; he is telling them who they are.

Whatever else this may mean, surely it means that *who* these people *are* is most important. Their personhood is the primary issue. As significant as their speech or deeds may subsequently be, it's their being, not their doing, that is most essential. Their intrinsic character, their integrity as disciples is to be open to all.

In a church I once served, there was a professor of fashion design who annually drafted a half-dozen men from the church to participate in a lineup for one of her classes. The challenge to her students was to see if they could guess each man's profession simply by observing his posture, face, and, of course, his dress. The first time I participated in this exercise, I dressed as I usually did on weekdays—in slacks and sport coat and tie. The students took one look at me and said, "You're a preacher." I hadn't opened my mouth, yet they "nailed" me. A couple of years later I again let myself be talked into participating in the lineup, but this time I dressed like a real "cool dude." The students studied me a bit longer but again concluded, "You're a preacher." What was the giveaway? My eyeglasses? My haircut? The fact I was just recovering from the flu? I still don't know.

What I uncomfortably felt in those fashion design lineups is perhaps an analogy for what Jesus had in mind as the identity of his followers. Who we are can't be in question for long. Something salty, something of the character of Jesus is detected. A salt-person brings a different flavor to the party, a flavor that can't be missed or mistaken. And through that distinctiveness the whole earth finds its hope.

But before some Jesus follower gets too euphoric about how important he or she is, we need to go back to the sobering center of this whole matter. Jesus spoke as though all of this is a *fait accompli*, a done deal. I can find only one plausible explanation for Jesus' preposterous conferring of salt status upon people he had to know were as knot-headed and self-centered as any of the rest of Adam's children: Jesus trusted God's transforming powers to be at work. He believed that by virtue of being with him they were and would be different, that rubbing shoulders with him would effect changes in their character. The commonest of clay could begin to radiate the luster of eternity because of proximity to Jesus. So he spoke from confidence in God, declaring this anticipated accomplishment of God as an already certain fact. "You *are* the salt of the earth, but not because of your moral superiority. You are salt because God is creating you so through me."

The significance of this is that moments spent with Jesus are the most essential moments of a disciple's life. Only in daily alertness before Jesus does the salty work of reshaping character occur. If these moments are omitted, if this communion is minimized, disciples become sad disappointments—containers labeled "Salt" but possessing only flavorless granules within.

And this brings us to the chapter's dreadful question: "If salt loses its taste, how can its saltiness be restored?"

Perhaps the chemists of the twenty-first century have developed a process for the re-salination of salt. I don't know. However, even if re-salination has or ever will become a possibility, Jesus' grim question still brings a shudder. When character, when distinctiveness and inner integrity are lost, what is left? Not much.

I'm told that the word for "losing saltiness" could just as reasonably have been translated "becoming foolish." I once saw such foolishness. It appeared in a church advertisement displaying a bearded male figure inviting readers to come and enjoy "Free Crackers and Grape Juice at My Dad's House." I cringed. Is it possible to reintroduce ultimacy, mystery, and transcendence once you have so cheaply made them cute? How can saltiness be restored once silliness has been chosen?

A lover of the church, writing from England, reminded his British audience that the nation's churches, though sadly abandoned, were actually its "only repositories of all-embracing meanings pointing beyond the immediate to the ultimate. They are the only institutions that deal in tears and concern themselves with the breaking points of human existence. As poet Philip Larkin said, they are 'serious places on serious earth.'"[1]

But Jesus' declaration turns that proud claim into a question: Is the church really "a serious place"? Lots of folks would say, "No, it's a superficial place, running from tears and side-stepping the breaking points of human existence."

Admittedly, Sundays spent churchgoing can be depressing experiences. Sometimes it's difficult to tell whether you're attending a worship service or a funeral, a motivational seminar, a political rally, a rock concert. Some of these programs may sell well for a season, but is there any salt within them? For myself, if what I encounter in a church isn't that different from what I hear anywhere else, I call it silliness. Granted, finding a Sunday place to rub shoulders with the character-changing Jesus, to hear his words, his deeds, and his manner of life held up seriously and winsomely for our emulation—that can be a tough search.

But wait, there's more! In our land we now have Christian movies, Christian bumper stickers, Christian novels, Christian tattoos, Christian music, Christian theme parks, Christian schools, Christian clothing—for all I know we may even have Christian dog food. But the Christ I read of in the New Testament surely can't be that popular. After all, they killed him, didn't they? It would appear that somebody has watered him down, sweetened him up, and leached even *his* saltiness.

Before the church can be the salt of this earth, it must confront Jesus' alternatives of integrity or irrelevance. Do we sincerely want to give unmistakable evidence that we are followers of an outcast? Of one who was unwanted two thousand years ago and is still trouble with a capital T when taken seriously?

I earlier confessed that I've often turned away from him, seeking refuge from the heat of his questions, and have loitered in the wings. Let me now add that even my times of hiding off stage have served to show me something significant: I've learned that I'm not too comfortable with God's grace. To be told "you are the salt of the earth" is a gift of God's grace, a promotion from anonymity to visibility. But that means it's a gift that places me and my life onto a larger, earth-sized stage. My spiritual comfort zone is invaded. Jesus defines me three sizes larger than I'd like. This is a gift I'd be happy to return to the Giver, but here it is—right in my face!

Grace, I'm learning, is more than mercy; it's also a compliment, an implicit affirmation. Grace means God thinks you are important, a desired partner in the enterprise of earth's redemption. Jesus' appearance among us showed this truth, and his salt-pronouncement inscripts it. Only our self-despising rejects it, playing inappropriately modest when God says, "Stand up and walk and talk and be the salt of this earth that I make of you!" One of discipleship's toughest tasks for me is to accept this compliment of God's grace. I am prepared for God's frown, but when I see a smile it frightens me. I shrink back, overwhelmed by this unexpected compliment—God's vote of confidence calling me to a higher self, a greater usefulness.

Living in the way of grace means we let Jesus define us. Not the demographers, not the sociologists, not the fashion-setters, nor the bankers or the educators or even our friends and family. We live into the self he sees and declares. We let him love the less-than-salty-self out of us—the worry, the fear, the pettiness, the anger. We let him groom the better stuff within. Day by day and choice by choice, we become what he says we are. If he once turned water into wine, surely it shouldn't be that impossible for him to make saving salt out of the likes of us.

In truth, I know it isn't impossible. I know it because I see it when I'm in the presence of some people. Often as not, regardless of what they are doing, it's *who they are* that attracts me. They are just different in a way that still feels right to call "the salt of the earth." And their very being persuades me that God, who is already wonderfully at work in some people, can enter into each of us and make us all who Jesus says we are.

Jesus, it's not that difficult for me to believe in you. But I'm still stunned when I consider that you might believe in me. I'm more comfortable being scolded than being crowned with glory and honor and given the chance to be an ambassador of the highest. But if you think it of me, let me not dismiss you and your word as being foolish. Spare me, Lord, from the regret of forfeited saltiness. Amen.

NOTE

1. David Martin, cited in John Young, *Teach Yourself Christianity* (Chicago: McGraw-Hill, 2003) 106. The Larkin poem referred to is "Church Going."

Chapter 9

A Question about War and Peace

"Do you think that I have come to bring peace to earth?"
(Luke 12:51)

One never knows the final outcome of any deed. A simple act, sometimes done without great expectations, can have consequences for good or for ill, far beyond one's imagination. A prime example from within the church's history is Martin Luther, who in 1517 drew up a list of ninety-five theological statements he believed worthy of debate. As the custom was in that day, he posted his list on the church doors, hoping to start some worthy discussion. He probably had no intention of pushing a first domino that would result in a division of western Christendom, but that's what happened.

By the same token, some outcomes we most fervently seek prove to be unreachable despite our best efforts. Three hundred years after Luther instigated the Reformation, a heartsick Danish Protestant, Søren Kierkegaard, devoted his literary skills to furthering Luther's reformation in the Danish church. The result? His genius is still admired and his writing skills are still studied, but his message created little more than a minor wrinkle on the church's smooth surface. That's not at all what he wanted.

So what of the intentions of the One who stands at the headwaters of this church? What did Jesus think he was up to? One persistent answer throughout the centuries has been that he came to bring peace on earth. Especially at Christmastime, the air drips with the sweetness of this idea.

Millions of pastel Christmas cards give the impression that an "all is calm, all is bright" peace is what Bethlehem was all about. But if

that's so, it certainly didn't feel or sound that way at the time. Not all
the scented candles and sweet lullabies of 2,000 Christmases can successfully muffle the cries of those mothers whose babies were soon
murdered by King Herod because of Bethlehem's silent, holy night
(Matt 2:16-18). If bringing peace on earth was Jesus' intention, his
pacification program had a tragic, grisly rollout.

It also appears that from the beginning, Jesus challenged the rosy
notion that his coming was meant to effect "peace on earth." He put
it in the form of a question, of course, but his own answer was swift
and clear. "Do you think I came to bring peace on earth? No, I tell
you. I came not to bring peace but a sword." I've yet to see that sting-
ing declaration printed on a Christmas card, although it's as much
about "peace on earth" as any of our happier verses. But who wants
to be told, especially when "Jingle Bells" is in the air, that even the
Prince of Peace doesn't have world peace stashed away on his sleigh?
Jesus, in fact, is on record as saying just the opposite.

So what do we do with such a shattering statement? If even Jesus
sidesteps the prospect of peace, to whom or to what shall we turn?

Fumbling about for some response, I start with the desirable
possibility that Jesus spoke this word sorrowfully rather than declar-
atively. Surely he was at least as wise as we are becoming, and he knew
that religious enmities are the worst enmities. Moreover, by offering
his understanding of God's will and way, he knew he would inevitably
become a source of division. Could it be, then, that Jesus' statement
is actually a word of sorrowful prophecy from one who knew human
nature well?

Karen Armstrong's many helpful writings in comparative religion
document how various religious streams often undergo a transformation from what she terms *mythos* to *logos*. *Mythos*, in her construal, is
the mythic, supra-historical "truth" lodged within each tradition. It
is its originating secret, its center of mystery, its revelatory insight,
and as such it is not subject to scientific analysis or to historical veri-
fication. *Logos*, on the other hand, is the rational, ordered, and precise
word of explanation extrapolated from the originating *mythos*. It is
the philosopher's fruit, the lawyer's code, not the mystic's wonder.
Armstrong maintains that when *logos* gains the upper hand in religion,

mythos suffers; the luminous "holy" becomes a specific creed and then a cause or a crusade, and eventually a persecutor if not a murderer of dissidents. Rather than being compelled by the moral vision of compassion or service of neighbor found within the *mythos*, devotees abandon concern for the neighbor and burrow down into *logos* crusades. Thus, what might have been a force for the world's betterment becomes yet another cause of division.[1]

Whatever credence one gives to Armstrong's understanding of faith's dynamics, it certainly isn't beyond belief that Jesus sorrowfully understood that regardless of his opposition to strife and violence, there would soon be "Christian" soldiers, fighting for the Jesus *logos*. Even before that devolution transpired, he understood that there would be families who would divide and shun and be shunned in his name.

Even so, surely it wasn't his intention. Can anyone seriously contend that Jesus wanted to create loss and destruction? He who would have nothing to do with calling down fire on his detractors— can he fairly be considered a zealot? He who stopped a vigilante execution squad in its tracks (John 8) and who cradled children in his arms—can he honestly be dubbed a friend of violence? Jesus' consistent record of relieving anguish gives no ground for such a conclusion. He was no closet sadist who gleefully anticipated inquisitorial fires being ignited in his wake. But he was realist enough to know that (1) he must speak his truth (*mythos*) as he understood it (or be false to himself); (2) humans consistently transform mystery into ideology; and therefore (3) peace would no more be his immediate legacy than it had or would be for any other truth teller.

A sidelight deserves closer inspection. A chasm does open when a person begins to attune his or her life's priorities to Jesus' upside-down valuation. A sword of division is thrust into any family, any group, when the rules are challenged. When that division happens, we can hope the group will distinguish between toxic fanaticism and robust faith. A comfortable religion of dull habit creates no division. Nor does it know how to deal with the passion of the true believer. In sum, interpersonal peace is not the first gift that vigorous faith brings.

It may well bring peace within, but all bets are off about its peaceful reception by others.

Another possible answer to this disturbing question of Jesus could be that it awakens us to the responsibility to be peacemakers. Not to be flippant about it, but if Jesus' question does no more than strip us of the excuse of "let George (that is, Jesus) do it," then it has served a grand purpose. It has put us on notice that we ourselves are the Lord's Peace Corps. This response would mean that Jesus' words are a plea for his followers to defy the predictable conversion of *mythos* to *logos* and to become people who would in his name become banner bearers for peace on earth.

Thankfully, this plea has been answered affirmatively across the centuries by many of his followers. Individuals like the Apostle Paul have preached a "gospel of peace" (Eph 6:15) and have given flesh to Jesus' "word of reconciliation" (2 Cor 5:19). Through their personal witness, social ministries, and diplomatic efforts, Christians have done much to diminish the countless animosities and the racial and cultural alienations of our world.

Still, for the most part, Jesus' plea to be peacemakers is a plea Christians have refused—and even returned it to the Sender. Rather than work for the peace we say we want, we've cleverly tasked God with that exhausting assignment. That way we can simultaneously claim impotence ("It's too difficult for us") and practice omnipotence ("Here, God, we delegate this to you").

It may be impossible to determine if Jesus was speaking sorrowfully or hopefully when he uttered this question. But his disturbing words do seem to suggest that violence and strife, like the poor, will always be with us—and that even God through Christ is not going to eradicate either until the final summing up.[2] In the case of poverty, the Scripture is clear that precisely *because* the poor will always be with us, we are always to be responsive to their needs. Similarly, precisely because violence and war will always be with us, we are always to be waging peace. The continuing presence of war is its own motivation to struggle for its end. But even as we struggle, we should be under no illusion that our efforts will eradicate violence and war any more than a war on poverty will eradicate poverty. Nonetheless, our very humanness, not to mention any possible allegiance to Jesus, insists that we work to mitigate poverty as well as violence and war.

For, to hazard a contrary view, who knows the final outcome of any of our deeds? Some word, some incident, some person's protest could be the catalyst for a societal shift as stunning as the one occasioned by Martin Luther. It will not do to give ourselves completely over to a posture of Kierkegaardian futility. To do so would be a tacit renunciation of hope in God.

Among the many stories told by veteran correspondent Chris Hedges in *War Is a Force that Gives Us Meaning*, there is one from the terror that was Bosnia in 1992. That story is of a Serbian couple, Rosa and Drago Sorak, who lived with their son Zoran and his pregnant wife in the city of Gorazde. Their city was besieged by the Bosnian Army; soon thereafter Zoran was arrested by Bosnian troops and taken away for questioning. He was never seen again.

In the now almost completely Muslim city, the situation of the Soraks became more desperate each day. At night they hid from roving vigilantes who sought to kill all Serbs; by day they stealthily foraged for scraps of food and materials to heat their small apartment. Nonetheless, with each passing week food shortages became more severe, and as a consequence infants, the elderly, and the infirm began to die. Five months into that hell, Zoran's wife gave birth to a little girl. The traumatized, starving mother was unable to nurse her newborn child. Drago and Rosa tried to sustain the little one with tea, but she began to fade.

Just before dawn on the child's fifth day of life, there was a quiet knock on their door. Warily opening it, Drago saw before him a Muslim man named Fejzic. Somehow, in spite of the war's cruelty, Fejzic had managed to preserve the life of a milk cow on a small lot at the edge of town. He milked it each night, in the dark of night, to avoid being gunned down by Serbian snipers. Now, in the dim light of dawn, he stood on the Soraks' doorstep, holding half a liter of milk in a container. Wordlessly he handed it up to Drago. He came the next morning and the next morning and the next. Other families began to notice and to scorn and threaten Fejzic for his kindness to the Serbian family and child. He offered no word of defense or rebuke to them, nor would he accept any pay from the despised Soraks. But for 442 days, he came with the half-liter of milk for the baby girl until the mother and infant finally were able to leave the city.

After this event the Soraks, despite their grief over their losses, would never allow other Serbs to speak unchallenged words about "the evil Muslims." They would quickly counter slanderous generalizations, insisting that others hear the story of Fejzic and his cow.

When the war concluded, Hedges located Fejzic, who then was living in another city—his own family, apartment, and cow lost to rampaging armies. His income consisted of the profits from peddling worm-eaten apples on the street, and his nights were spent in an unheated room shared with several other men. But when Hedges told him he'd seen the Soraks, Fejzic's eyes brightened. "And the baby?" he asked. "How is she?"

Chris Hedges sees "an ocean of hope" in the action of this illiterate farmer. "The small acts of decency by people such as . . . Fejzic . . . in wartime ripple outwards like concentric circles," Hedges wrote. "They serve as reminders that we all have a will of our own, a will that is independent of the state or the nationalist cause. Most important, once the war is over, these people make it hard [for others] to brand an entire nation or an entire people as guilty." And perhaps more important: "By accepting that they [the Soraks] could only affect a few lives they also accepted their small place in the universe. This daily lesson in humility protected them. They were saved not by what they could accomplish but by faith."[3]

Stories like this, reporting "small acts of decency," are routinely dismissed as sentimentally nice but sadly lacking in an orientation to reality. "Small acts of decency" are said to be politically ineffective in altering injustice or halting aggression. Perhaps that is so. Who can deny the strength of that opinion? But can't the same response be made to those who champion the effectiveness of war and violence as antidotes to injustice? Have war and violence ever been so successful in stanching evil? Have they not just as often created new situations of international ill will while introducing new weaponry and countless unforeseen negative consequences? War may rearrange the scenery for a while—and in the face of great evil it may even be deemed tragically necessary—but history repetitiously documents the long-term futility of war as a final solution to the evil we oppose.

Fejzic's story documents that personal acts of peacemaking do bear fruit. They are more than sentimentally nice; there is within them "an ocean of hope," especially when compared to the piled-high bodies of a thousand wars. Liters of milk offered to "enemies" contain more promise of peace than all the armaments of the world.

But for this to be anything more than pious wishing, the followers of the Prince of Peace must be more militant in waging peace. That effort might begin, as Chris Hedges suggests, by being less concerned for what we can accomplish than for what we can say through faith-full deeds. This might be something as simple and yet as difficult as listening to another. To offer open ears to those with whom we disagree is a godly gift. To it we might add the preposterous things Jesus said to do, like turning cheeks, going second miles, and answering cursing with blessing—not because they are sure to transform the antagonist but because in the doing of them a faithful replica of Christ has been given. "On the last day of the world / I would want to plant a tree," wrote W. S. Merwin, poetically capturing the Christian's admittedly hopeless yet completely hopeful battle strategy.[4]

I realize my words can possibly be interpreted as unpatriotic or disrespectful of the countless men and women who have risked or lost their lives fighting for the freedom that allows me to express my views. I regret this because I am most respectful of those who serve my nation militarily. Because I do respect them so profoundly, I want fewer of them to return home in flag-draped caskets. I want fewer of them to carry the physical and emotional wounds of war for the balance of their lives. I want my nation and the nations of this world to invest their wealth in the quality of their citizens' lives rather than in the stockpiling of weaponry. I want the world's children to be freed from the idiotic fantasy that violence settles things. No doubt these desires are impossible dreams. And perhaps the desire that's even more impossible is to have Christians measure the gulf between our professed loyalty to Jesus and our silent acceptance, if not endorsement, of the way of violence and war. But surely, before followers of the Lamb march off to kill others, we need to ask if this war must be.

One of my most memorable parade-watching moments came on a Veteran's Day as I stood on the sidewalk of a county-seat town. For the better part of an hour I watched a colorful procession of high school bands, clowns, Shriners' go-carts, military weaponry, veterans groups, tanks, local politicians tossing candies from loaned convertibles, honor guards, and 4-H floats. It was a stirring sight, a fitting expression of gratitude for the nation's military, and it came at a time when our national war-fever was high. But, at the end of the parade, just in front of the fire truck that was the standard ending piece in our local parades, was a small group of middle-aged men. As I remember it, all were dressed in street clothes, but the banner they carried declared their purpose and their identity: "STOP THE WAR— Veterans for Peace." No blood-stirring band preceded these contrarian patriots; they walked in solemn silence, the tailpiece of the parade.

Correction: There was an accompanying soundtrack for them. As they marched past me, a trio of low-flying military fighter jets soared just above our main street, their deafening roar and intimidating power causing me to cringe and duck.

Opening my eyes again, I realized I knew the fellow leading the group. Charlie. We were members of the same Rotary Club. We'd talked a time or two over lunch at a club meeting, but the only things I knew about Charlie was that he was an intelligent, decorated veteran with an impressive military background. He knew his leadership in this demonstration would cost him. And he knew his witness for peace wasn't likely going to change the course of history. But there he was, uttering his public, unmistakable "No!" to violence and to war.

I don't know Charlie's religious affiliation—or even if he had any. But when I think of what it means to follow Jesus, Charlie's lonely walk still comes to mind.

Jesus, I am so very, very tired of war. But violence is everywhere: the box-office does best when fiery explosions and mangled bodies fill the screen; the crowds flock to see men in fenced rings beat and kick one another senseless; the wild west days of "packing heat" have returned—today's newspaper tells me that Americans now have nine guns for every ten people, and even the church youth group plays laser-tag war games. Lord, we are addicted to "shoot 'em up" violence, hardened to cheap death. By the kindness of your cross, coax the swords, especially the religious ones, from our hands and teach us how to use these hands gently, firmly, for life and for hope. Amen.

Notes

1. See Karen Armstrong, *The Battle for God: A History of Fundamentalism* (New York: Ballantine Books, 2000) for this development.

2. A good case has been made by Steven Pinker in *The Better Angels of Our Nature: Why Violence Has Declined* (New York: Viking Penguin Group, 2011) that I am being unduly pessimistic in this assessment. Others who are waging the battles against poverty and hunger also may be disappointed in my apparent defeatism. My larger point, however, is not so much an attempt to foretell the future as it is to urge unrelenting opposition to these wrongs, regardless of the uneven historical success of such opposition.

3. Chris Hedges, *War Is a Force that Gives Us Meaning* (New York: Anchor Books, 2002) 53, 49ff.

4. W. S. Merwin, "Place," in *The Rain in the Trees* (New York Alfred A. Knopf, 1988).

Chapter 10

A Question about Government

*"Why are you putting me to the test? Bring me a
denarius and let me see it. . . . Whose head is this,
and whose title?" (Mark 12:15-16)*

When I was a seminarian I was told that if I should ever venture to
preach on a controversial and especially a political topic, I ought to
prepare a complete manuscript and not depart from it. The objective
was to build a safeguard so that no politically incensed listener might
be able to misquote me. Even at that tender age, it seemed to me that
the unspoken truth admitted in this counsel was that political issues,
not theological claims, were where listeners' passions resided. I concluded, in perhaps an immature hastiness, that I could safely serve up
any off-the-cuff drivel about God, but I must be extremely careful if
I dared say anything about Democrats, Republicans, public policy, or
political matters. Politics was high-voltage, sacrosanct turf embedded
with land mines. Theology, on the other hand, was tame territory—
unless, of course, one preached the nonexistence of hell or denied the
virgin birth.

As sobering as that early conclusion was, it put modern-day dress
on the ancient duel between the powers that be and the Power that
Is. The Bible documents this struggle repeatedly, telling story after
story of the clash between prophets of God and rulers of earthly king-
doms. It's the basis for the fiery confrontation between the prophet
Elijah and the king and queen of Israel (Ahab and Jezebel)—resulting
in Elijah running for his life and the royal couple coming to no good
end (1 Kings 16ff). It's the fire fueling the prophet Amos's scalding
rebuke of the rich elites, and it's the smoke behind the rage of the
king's chaplain ordering Amos out of the country. It's also why John
the Baptist's head was served up on a platter.

One place it appears in Jesus' ministry is in a politically loaded question fired at him by his detractors. The Gospel writer makes it clear that their query was maliciously intended; they had been sent "to trap him in what he said" (Mark 12:12). Their desire was to get him to incriminate himself with the occupying Roman armies and authorities as a tax evader who was teaching others to do the same. "Is it lawful to pay taxes to the emperor or not?" they asked. If he answered "No," the powers that be had the proof they sought; if he answered "Yes," many of his followers would be displeased with his apparent collaboration with the Roman occupiers.

Jesus answered by asking them to present to him a coin, the kind used to pay the unpopular (and to some religious minds, blasphemous) taxes. Drawing attention to the engraving on the coin, he asked, "Whose head is this, and whose title?" When they replied that the Roman emperor's head and title appeared on the coin, Jesus deftly stepped out of their net by saying, "Give to the emperor the things that are the emperor's and to God the things that are God's."

His masterful Houdini trick worked: his questioners "were utterly amazed at him" and asked no follow-up questions. But two thousand years later, it's impossible not to press the issue further and ask what Jesus might have meant by this now famous Caesar and God statement, and not simply as a matter of historical curiosity. Is there help here for our continuing search for the proper relationship between citizenship and religious faith?

One time-honored interpretation of these words says that Jesus here divides the world into two spheres, the secular and the religious. Some things belong to God and other things belong to the emperor. Honor the difference and give to each what is his due and all will be well. Much of the New Testament squares up with this endorsement of compliance with the powers that be. No less an authority than the Apostle Paul instructed the Christians in Caesar's own city, Rome, as follows:

> Let every person be subject to the governing authorities; for there is no authority except from God, and those authorities that exist have been instituted by God. Therefore whoever resists authority

resists what God has appointed, and those who resist will incur judgment. For rulers are not a terror to good conduct, but to bad. Do you wish to have no fear of the authority? Then do what is good, and you will receive its approval, for it is God's servant for your good. But if you do what is wrong, you should be afraid, for the authority does not bear the sword in vain! It is the servant of God to execute wrath on the wrongdoer. Therefore one must be subject, not only because of wrath but also because of conscience. For the same reason you also pay taxes, for the authorities are God's servants, busy with this very thing. Pay to all what is due them—taxes to whom taxes are due, revenue to whom revenue is due, respect to whom respect is due, honor to whom honor is due. (Rom 13:1-7)

In another letter there is an injunction to offer "supplications, prayers, intercessions, and thanksgivings . . . for kings and all who are in high positions . . ." (1 Tim 2:1-2), and in another place Christians are told, "For the Lord's sake accept the authority of every human institution, whether of the emperor as supreme, or of governors, as sent by him to punish those who do wrong and to praise those who do right" (1 Pet 2:13-14, 17).

These texts share the approach of the two spheres of interpreting Jesus' words. They see no clash between good citizenship and good faith. Fortunately, there are historical instances when our government and God can be faithfully and simultaneously served. The age of the apostles was largely such a time—a time when the *Pax Romana* granted unprecedented liberty and safety for travel (and therefore for the dissemination of the Christian message). This is the societal backdrop for the passages in the New Testament that urge compliance and prayer and honor be given to those in authority.

However, one of the difficulties of this two-sphere approach became apparent several centuries later when kings and emperors used it to legitimize their often-cruel use of power. They claimed that if Jesus had said to "give to the emperor what is due the emperor," then obviously Jesus had no problem with emperors or with their demands. Monarchs, therefore, regardless of the manner in which they exercised their power, claimed to rule by divine right and to have legitimate right to demand what they wished. "To resist the king is to resist God!" the argument went, and it was a most powerful argument— especially when backed up by dungeons, torture racks, and chaplains who excused the sovereign's bloodiest deeds with politically deft maneuvers or simply looked the other way.

The fact, however, is that the problems within a two-sphere concept were evident long before this. Where does one draw the line between Caesar's things and God's things? Elijah and Amos for example were not, to our knowledge, law-breakers or disrupters of the peace of the land, and if there were taxes due to the rulers of their day we have no indication that they were not paying them. They, in effect, gave to the earthly ruler the things that were due him. Everything, that is, except silence in the face of evil royal policies. At this point they gave to God the things that belong to God—like ultimate loyalty demonstrated in speech and action even against the powers that be.

Later, when Jesus' disciples Peter and John were commanded by the powers that be to cease their preaching concerning Jesus, they defiantly replied, "Whether it is right in God's sight to listen to you rather than to God, you must judge; for we cannot keep from speaking about what we have seen and heard" (Acts 4:19-20). Peter and John continued preaching, and both men paid dearly for it. According to tradition, Caesar's men eventually strung up Peter by his heels and exiled John to the isle of Patmos where, in his famous revelation, he declared that the earthly ruler who had "power . . . throne . . . and great authority" was nothing less than a beast from the belly of hell (Rev 13:1ff).

So the meaning of Jesus' famous Caesar and God comment can't be ticketed off with an easy "keep both sides happy" approach. That idea extends only so far, and then it becomes apparent that there aren't two spheres for our living: secular and religious. Life is one reality, one sphere that includes all we do and are. There are no "things" that can rightly be deemed solely Caesar's. Whether we are speaking about taxes or sex or baseball, all these seemingly secular matters have their sacred import. Taxes have to do with fairness and the common good; these are religious matters. Sex has to do with personhood and respect; these are religious matters. Even baseball has to do with rules and with play; once again, sacred themes are involved. The point here is that life is of one piece; all of life is sacred because all of life is a gift from God, and we are accountable to God for every bit of it. All of it, politics and government just as surely as religion and church, is to reflect the will of God the giver.

(It may turn out that Jesus' use of the coin was a brilliant way of saying that this coin shows the face and name of its issuer: Caesar. So give it back to him—it is his. And, conversely, you show that you bear the image and name of God. So give back to God the self that you are; you are God's!)

What validity or wisdom can be gleaned for today from Jesus' clever question and answer about Caesar and God? What guidance remains in it—if any—for negotiating the claims of God and government? Supremely, I note that Jesus did not disparage Caesar but spoke of him as one to whom honor is due. In this, Jesus doesn't confer upon Caesar a status equal to God, but he does assert the legitimacy of human government. Despite the many instances of abuse and oppression that history's rulers provide, government is necessary, and good government is as essential to the functioning of society as is good religion.

There is then no inherent reason that a faithful Christian cannot serve God as well in the political realm as in any other. Although it has sometimes been held that politics is too sordid a business for Christian involvement, such a statement has no more consistency than a Christian medical doctor's refusal to treat sick people because they have too many germs. Indeed, if politics is essentially how a society determines who gets what, when, and how, then few arenas offer more opportunities to "love thy neighbor as thyself" than politics.

Unfortunately, popular opinion frequently ranks politicians only a stripe or two above, if not in the same category as, con men. Some North Carolinians, for example, enjoy the story about a certain Senator Strange who ordered that his tombstone not state his name but bear only a five-word inscription: *Here Lies an Honest Politician.* The stonemason objected, "But, Senator Strange, how are passersby going to know it's your grave?" "Well," explained the senator, "when they read those five words, the first thing they're going to say is, "Now, that's strange!"

Sadly, the only thing such tales tell us is that politics is one of the many arenas of human service where more people of honesty are sorely needed. I'm sure there are currently many people of true integrity within the political arena. Our great need is for more of them.

That being said, history has given us too many examples of how people of faith can also pollute the political waters so as to make them nearly non-potable. It is one thing to serve God *in* the political arena; it is a far different (and ignoble) thing to pretend to *be* God in the political arena. My own Eight Commandments (I'm not smart enough to come up with ten) for Politically Active Believers could, if followed, spare us from many of these embarrassing instances—and supply worthy substance to those confrontations that discipleship continues to make necessary.

1. Thou shalt believe in original sin. No facet of life escapes the blight of sin and no political viewpoint is pure and free from bias or error, even your own.

2. Thou shalt not be a one-issue activist; society's well-being is multi-faceted.

3. Thou shalt not bear false witness. Winning by smearing is a loss.

4. Thou shalt do thy homework. Quoting the Bible is permissible, but only if you've studied the issues and can cite other reputable authorities as well.

5. Thou shalt not neglect the poor or blame them for their poverty.

6. Thou shalt not trample on religious freedom or the religious views of others.

7. Thou shalt not whine when attacked by media or foes. Politics is a contact sport, proving once again that loving one's neighbor isn't child's play.

8. Thou shalt remember that "God 'n country" is *not* one word.

Political speech often drips with religious overtones, candidates and parties eager to clothe themselves in pure messianic garments. From this posturing it is only a short step for citizens to confer upon the nation itself the aura of divinity, ascribing to its policies the authority and blessing of the Almighty. Such thoughtless patriotism mistakes an appropriate love of one's country for an idolatrous deification of it. Given the lush religious associations to be found in our relatively young nation's history, this is an easy error to make. But our founders, being only one or two generations away from the horrors of Europe's bloody and protracted "religious" wars, were very aware of the dangers of uniting the powers of religion with the powers of state. As a bulwark against an American repetition of this error, they adopted what some have called a "godless" Constitution, that is, a Constitution that forbade any religious tests for governmental service and that outlawed any federal establishment of religion or prohibition of its free exercise. In subsequent years this legacy has been called the policy of separation of church and state. In its inception, it was just smart public policy. It still is!

Religion and politics will inevitably intersect. How could it be otherwise, if both are concerned with the proper administration of our life together? Admitting the inevitable (and even desirable) interface of religion and politics is not the same thing as endorsing a union of the institution we call the state and the institution we call the church. When church and state are intermingled, our democratic society forfeits an unofficial fourth form of our prized system of "checks and balances." The voice of righteous criticism and principled praise is muzzled when these institutions lose their separateness.

The short and sufficient creed for the earliest church was "Jesus is Lord." That assertion, however, was not just a theological pronouncement. It was also a political statement, a pledge of ultimate loyalty to someone other than Caesar. While the rest of the Roman Empire obediently said, "Caesar is Lord," these Christians insisted that for them Jesus, not Caesar, was Lord. Predictably, the Caesars punished such dissent. We're now centuries and oceans away from those early days of Christianity, but the necessary tension between the powers that be and the Power that Is remains.

Psalm 23 speaks of green pastures and still waters for the faithful. But for those who deal with politics—which arguably includes every one of us who is a citizen of this nation—briar patches and opponents' barbs are also part of the package. One can only hope that some of the scratches we receive come from standing for the issues Jesus placed in the forefront.

Jesus, when I pray "thy kingdom come, thy will be done on earth as it is in heaven," I'm actually praying a political prayer, am I not? It's easy to forget that things like daily bread and discerning who trespassed against whom are at the heart of politics as well as of life. Help me learn to love my neighbor in this way also, Lord. And keep me from giving my heart away to any loyalty less than you—even to my so-called Christian country. For your kingdom's sake, help me keep God and Caesar separate, but always talking to one another. Amen.

Chapter 11

A Question about Jesus and You

"But who do you say that I am?" (Mark 8:29)

Although I've always cared what others think of me, I don't recall ever asking anyone to tell me their opinion about me. That's a bolder request than I've ever felt comfortable making. More typically, the verdicts of others are reserved for retirement parties or funeral eulogies, even though neither of these occasions is known for the highest level of candor. So it's striking that Jesus would press the issue, point blank, with his disciples.

He has just asked what others were saying about him—a safe enough testing of the PR winds—but then he boldly confronts them about their own assessments: "Who do you say that I am?" It's a cornering question with no wiggle room.

From the standpoint of good manners, Jesus can be frowned upon for pressing the question. But his purpose compensates for whatever he may be lacking in American middle-class manners. Through this blunt question we're reminded that, contrary to our infatuation with freedom, life isn't found by keeping all options open, by forming no deep convictions or allegiances. When Jesus asks his disciples to declare their opinion of him, he is pushing them toward careful thought and self-definition. I don't think it's ego that prompts Jesus to be assertive here. It's a ministry question: "Have I yet communicated to you my true identity and therefore the astonishing mercy of the God I represent?" It's also a question driven by compassion: "Have you yet reached clarity in your own minds about who you now are and the life implications of what you have seen and heard?" Being pressed to grapple with matters of ultimate significance—including one's opinion of Jesus—builds maturity.

For some of us, an answer to Jesus' question was given with our mother's milk. Stories and picture books about the little baby Jesus, his going about doing good, and his eventual death and resurrection have been with us since our infancy. We were told that Jesus is the Son of God who came to die for our sins and was raised from death so we could live eternally. We were expected to believe this, and many of us did. Others of us were fed no such understanding of Jesus; what we know we picked up in bits and pieces from sources as varied as *Jesus Christ, Superstar* to televangelists or roommates who "got religion." Regardless of where or how our understanding of Jesus began, most of us come to a day when we're no longer content with inherited faith or no faith. We want to sift the evidence for ourselves and come to our own conclusions, to do exactly what Jesus asked his disciples to do. To speak for ourselves.

In my case, I identify greatly with the little boy who complained, as he was ordered to go wash his hands, that all they ever talked about in his home was germs and Jesus—and he'd never seen either one. Lots of personal wrestling, intellectual as well as emotional and spiritual, marked my movement from a childhood impression of Jesus as God's boy who was punished for the naughty things I had done, to my present understanding of him: the incomparable One who reveals the face of God in all its Calvary-stained glory, making possible a grateful, trusting response to this God.

In fact, the word "incomparable" is one of my favorites as an answer to Jesus' question. You don't need a PhD or three months in a monastery to understand this word. The gospel story (in Mark 8) says that Simon Peter used an entire sentence to answer Jesus' question: "You are the Christ, the son of the living God." As the rest of that conversation reveals, however, Peter was using an unmastered vocabulary, throwing out heavy words that carried a theological freight he didn't understand. So, with a thank-you for the contributions made by the theologian's heavy terms (like "hypostatic union," "begotten not made," "monophysite" and "monothelite," etc.), I am content to restrict myself to saying that Jesus is simply incomparable. It's not that

I disbelieve the big words or the theological terms; it's just that when I imagine myself in Peter's shoes, I can't see myself using them. They are good words, clarifying words for analytical moments, but frankly I've seldom seen such words wear a smile. And they always need a paragraph-long definition. So something like "You are incomparable" sounds about right for my answer—or at least my initial answer.

This word feels appropriate for me on several levels. For one thing, I find the historical person of Jesus to be incomparable. His life story is different enough to merit that term. The outward contours of that story, sorrowfully, are not so different from that of many people, especially those born into subjugated circumstances. In Jesus' case, this meant he was born in peasant surroundings, grew up in obscurity, and was executed in his early thirties as a criminal. There's nothing unique within this tragic plot line; many others share it with Jesus. Jesus' incomparability emerges only when we consider that "he never traveled more than ninety miles from his birthplace, owned nothing, attended no college, marshaled no army, and instead of producing books did his only writing in the sand. Nevertheless, as George Buttrick once said, 'his birthday is kept across the world and his death day sets a gallows against most every skyline.'"[1]

In addition to this striking life story, I am also perpetually impressed by how Jesus lived: the way he dealt with his friends and treated his enemies, the way he handled daily disappointments and relentless challenges, his courage and his wisdom, the way he trusted God even to the depth of Golgotha—is there a parallel to it anywhere or in any other religion? Judaism has Moses and Islam Mohammed, yet these great individuals give only teachings to follow. They do not offer themselves as the model to follow. In Jesus' revealing life I find a credible model, an instructor as well as instructions. He does more than describe the good life; he lives it before us and then says, "Follow me." This I judge to be historically incomparable. (And even if I'm sadly mistaken here, God surely can't be disappointed, nor will I be a fool, for my having chosen such a model.)

But in making such claims about Jesus, I realize I must give some reply to those who are skeptical about the truthfulness of what's said in the Gospels about him. Each year, and often just before Easter, publishers release yet another book challenging the credibility of the New Testament accounts. One of the more recent of these suggested that Jesus was married rather than celibate as the New Testament would lead us to believe. Not to be forgotten is the cluster of books coming from the famous *Jesus Seminar*, which made front-page news, less for the opinions of the scholars involved as for the way each scholar registered her or his opinion—by casting a marble of various-coded colors for whether a particular saying of Jesus was judged to be *certainly* his, *probably* his, or *certainly not* his. The hype surrounding books like this gives the impression that these scholars' opinions are scandalously new. In fact, the challenge of historical skepticism has been with us for centuries, and any good introductory textbook on the New Testament sketches the history of this issue and the scholars and theories integral to it.[2]

When I was first introduced to this information, it was deeply upsetting. After all, from infancy onward all I'd heard about was the Jesus presented on the pages of my New Testament, the one whose words I could read in red print. I did not question that these words were the exact words of Jesus. But once I was confronted by the historical skepticism of others—and their reasons for it—I knew I had to deal with such skepticism honestly. This is not the place to reconstruct the search that then became mine, but perhaps it is the place for me to state where I finally landed.

I now see no need or much benefit in attempting to prove that every detail of the Gospels happened just as it is stated. That's because I no longer measure the Gospels' authors by the yardstick I use when I am reading the work of today's historians. I now think that while the Gospel writers did not simply invent interesting Jesus stories out of sanctified imagination, neither did they write impartial biographies of the man named Jesus. Objective historical reporting was not their purpose. The Gospel writers were preaching on parchment, heralding a discovery about this man Jesus. They'd encountered a wonder in Jesus of Nazareth that defied any category they knew. That new category was God-in-human-flesh, and in response they wrote a distinct kind of narrative literature. The writers of these Gospels took the treasured memories of the eyewitnesses of Jesus' ministry and wove them into a consecutive story about Jesus, a story told to preserve the memories for coming generations and to persuade others to share this amazing discovery and join in the Jesus movement. As John says, "These things are written so that you may believe" (20:31), not that you might have an impartial chronicler's account of each conversation, deed, and date of Jesus' life.

Concluding that historical exactitude wasn't the aim of the Gospels doesn't mean, however, that we can't trust the truth of their portrait of Jesus. One might consider here the difference between an artist's portrait and a photographer's image of a person. The photograph may let you count the exact number of wrinkles on the subject's face, but the artist's portrait will often give you a better impression of the personality of the subject. The Gospel-writing "artists" didn't foist on us a cartoon; they "painted" a trustworthy portrait of Jesus. Even if the Gospel writers took what we today might call liberties with details, they nonetheless told the truth about him. They were attempting to tell of his meaning, not the minutiae of each day's activities. In doing so they provided a true representation of the man and his significance for all generations.

Some who wrestle with these matters are also troubled when they reckon with the fact that no one was there with audio-video equipment or even with a stenographer's notebook as Jesus spoke. How then do we know what Jesus actually said? Their concern may even be heightened when they notice the difference between the speech of Jesus in the Gospel of John and his speech in the other three Gospels. John's Jesus uses a stylized vocabulary (light/darkness; life/death; love/hate) and a manner of speaking (in lengthy paragraphs that sound almost repetitiously convoluted upon first reading) that is very different from the staccato, action-oriented speech of Mark's Jesus, the discursive, didactic speech of Matthew's Jesus, or the storytelling genius of Luke's Jesus. Such notable differences lead some readers to wonder if the Gospel writers used their own speech patterns and vocabularies rather than his.

Add to this the fact that Jesus spoke Aramaic but our Gospel writers all wrote their manuscripts in Greek. Centuries later, copies of their Greek manuscripts were translated into English by multiple translators. This means the words of Jesus that appear in our English New Testaments have already gone through two translational challenges, from Aramaic to Greek and from Greek to English. Now, even a rudimentary knowledge of the distinctiveness of languages awakens us to the near impossibility of providing a word-for-word translation from one language to another. Often the two languages and cultures can be so dissimilar that a word-for-word translation will be nonsensical to the new reader. So the translator's only option is to risk the best approximation of the original he or she can—with a success rate none but God can know. (The grim side of this forms the basis for the Italian saying, *traduttore tradittorre*, meaning "the translator is a traitor.")

Where does this bring us in our search for the precise words spoken by Jesus? If we understand that the Gospel writers' intent wasn't to provide us with transcripts of every conversation or event-by-event reconstructions of each day, the Gospels are best understood as historically based sermons. We may wish we had "objective" biographical studies like David McCullough's *Truman* or Walter Isaacson's *Einstein*, but in this case it's just not possible because we don't have the source materials. Thus, we operate with what we have (Gospels, good news tracts), and we accept them on their own terms as being the literature of advocacy, not modern biography.

This means, to me, that it's unwise to insist that the historical Jesus said, word for word, every statement attributed to him in the New Testament. On the other hand, I believe we have far more direct quotations of Jesus than many skeptics claim, and I also believe that what we read in the Gospels is a faithful representation of the man and his words, even if often presented to us through the voice and vocabulary of the Gospel writers.

Scholars of the era of Jesus are united in saying that the people of his day relied, by necessity, on the powers of oral tradition and memory much more than we can imagine. Literacy was the exception rather than the rule of that day. Therefore, individuals' ability to remember specifics was as marked as is our dependence on technology to do the same for us. I don't, therefore, find it incredible that Jesus' listeners could reconstruct from memory many of his actual sentences, and certainly his arresting one-liners and intriguing questions. The reliability of their recall is made even more plausible if we give any credence to the aid of the Holy Spirit as a helper in their work.

To those whose doubts about this matter continue, I ask them to consider the likelihood that a person and a message like that of Jesus of Nazareth could really have been the creation of four mortals: Matthew, Mark, Luke, and John. I cannot believe that these four simply concocted someone so unconventional, so wise, and so powerful. Nor can I believe that any four mortals, without some form of divine assistance, could have written up Jesus' story in such a manner that two thousand years later we are still drawn to and dumbfounded by this Jesus and what he said, did, and suffered for us.

So, even if I concede the possibility that there could be differences between what Jesus actually said and what appears in red letters in some editions of the New Testament, I am confident that those red letters don't misrepresent Jesus. To me, this is *very* important! Those red-letter sentences convey to us what the resurrected, living Jesus wants us to hear today; they are from him, for us. Stated differently, the English words now before us represent what God would have us hear *today* as "the word of the Lord" Jesus. So the issue isn't so much what Jesus *said* as it is what Jesus *is saying* to us through these texts. In this respect, I may be more of a believer in the Holy Spirit's work than some of my more theologically conservative friends. For I believe God's Holy Spirit not only assisted the memory faculties of the eyewitnesses but also guided the creative literary efforts of the Gospel writers as they wrote. I also believe this same Spirit presided over the amazing preservation of the copied manuscripts through the centuries and the eventual translations of them into the languages of the world. The result is that these Gospels present us with a portrait of Jesus and his message that, like everything else about Jesus, is reliable, surprising, and incomparable. Those words in red are what the living Jesus is saying to the church and world *now*. I could not have written this book nor continued in Christian ministry for half a century without this life-giving conviction.

When we read the Gospels with appreciation for their unique purpose and according to the conventions of writing history that were then in operation, we have no reason to discredit them as trustworthy guides to the person and message of the One who once lived in Palestine, the One who continues to live and speak through these documents, the One causing the truth of God's word to ring through the Gospel stories to this very hour. When I read the Gospels in this way, I see a man, Jesus of Nazareth, who is in amazing communion with God, vitally in touch with an unseen world of power and wisdom. That contact brimmed over into words and deeds that still astound us. The man himself lived with a humility and compassion that eclipses every other prophet or religious leader I know of. In him there was no bluster, no ego-need, no meanness of spirit, no dilettante's arrogance. In him was life—and that life was the light for all of us—but it was a light he didn't flaunt or push on anyone. In all this, I find the man himself to be incomparable. The truth is, I cannot speak of Jesus as just a historical figure. In a personal and practical way, he is as real to me today as you are.

Let me illustrate my meaning by telling you about my prayers. I begin with this confession: I am not the one to consult if you are seeking counsel about how to establish a daily period of prayer. That discipline has proven itself invaluable over centuries to multitudes of people, and I must commend it. It is with embarrassment that I cannot claim to practice it daily. The fact is my prayers are more of the sentence and conversational type that occur at unnumbered times throughout the day. A lot of people admit to talking to themselves at times—and I do some of that, too—but just as often, I talk to Jesus. Were you standing beside me during one of those moments, you'd likely think I'm exceedingly weird—and indeed that may be so!—but Jesus is as lively and accessible to me as any living person. The sight of a child at play or a beggar at the roadside or the news of someone's suffering is sufficient to get me talking to Jesus. I have no other such companion.

The same conclusion comes when I open the Bible and sincerely seek to be spoken to through its words. Put a rationalistic gloss on this if you wish, but often it is as though a living voice speaks to me from the printed page, and I call that personal tutor the living spirit of Jesus. Certainly there are many times when I pore over chapters of

Scripture and wade through dusty biblical research volumes and hear not so much as a peep. I have learned, however, that even those dreary, silent hours train me to detect this voice all the more clearly in the moments when he does speak.

If you want to tell me Jesus of Nazareth is rotting in a Jerusalem tomb, you might as well save your breath. I've had too many conversations with him to buy it. (And, yes, there have been times across the years when I'd almost swear he was talking back to me, like a true conversation partner.)

Through all the years of my life, whatever my circumstance has been, Jesus has always been pertinent. A story remembered from childhood is applicable here. It was about a boy who was shooting backyard basketball hoops when some neighborhood bullies walked by, roughed him up, and stole his basketball. He ran home, crying that he was such a helpless wimp. His older brother overheard his crying and came to his room, asking what was the matter. The boy shared his story of humiliation. Minutes later he was in the bullies' backyard, bravely declaring, "I came to get my ball back." Then, pointing to his brother standing at his side, he said, "And this time I brought my big brother!" Even when I was a boy, this story reminded me of Jesus—my thorn-crowned older brother who stands alongside me, against all of life's bullies.

My days of boyhood are long gone, but the brother is still here. When the bully I face is temptation, I find that Jesus has also had to deal with the tempter (Mark 4). When the bully is confusion and weariness, Jesus' promise to give rest to exhausted souls proves true (Matt 11). When the bully is the stain of failure and the weight of guilt, I've discovered, as a gospel song puts it, "He took my sins and my sorrows and made them his very own; he took the burden to Calvary and suffered and died alone."[3] Even when the bully will one day be Death, I'm relying on this older brother not to abandon me but to come and take me where he is (John 14).

(None of this is to deny that there are days when I am unaware of Jesus' presence, days when life proceeds without much conversation between us. Perhaps that's sinful in some folks' opinion. In my own estimation, it can also be called an indication of a trusted friendship;

I don't need to reassure myself constantly that he is "with and for me." None of this testimony, however, is to deny or to mock the testimony of others I'll consider in the next chapter, people for whom the absence of God is an agonizing problem.)

It may be that you are surprising yourself as you read these words. Perhaps religion hasn't been your thing. As you've read my assessment of Jesus, it could be that you find yourself incredulous or perhaps disgusted or envious. That's how it goes, friend. One man's treasure is another man's trash. But I couldn't write this book without including my testimony and a final declaration: Jesus is the heart-, the soul-, the gut-deep friend I have needed. To know him personally, to be able to speak with him as a living friend, to feel his gentle steel steadying me when everything else is crumbling—this is salvation. And I believe it is a salvation that is possible for everyone who will open themselves to his presence and merciful guidance. He truly is incomparable.

That's my response. But what about you? Who do you say he is?

Jesus, you've been a part of my thought world since childhood. I've grown up with you. But I thank you that you've become more than biographical scenery to me; you've become central, and that gives me peace and hope even when I'm running on empty. I don't know if there's anything worth calling salvation to be found in other ways or faiths. I do know I find you incomparable, and for this I am most grateful. If it pleases you, use my story to help someone else discover that you are so much more than just another religious figure. Amen.

NOTES

1. Huston Smith, *The Religions of Man* (New York: Harper & Row Perennial Library, 1958) 266–67.

2. A useful overview of the more recent books, authors, and issues can be found in Ben Witherington III's *The Jesus Quest: The Third Search for the Jew of Nazareth*, new expanded edition (Downers Grove IL: Intervarsity Press, 1997). A judicious biblical/theological synthesis and personal conclusion has been written by the venerated New Testament scholar Leander E. Keck: *Who Is Jesus? History in Perfect Tense* (Minneapolis: Fortress Press, 2001). Witherington and Keck both offer

excellent bibliographies for further study. Luke Timothy Johnson, *The Real Jesus: The Misguided Quest for the Historical Jesus and the Truth of the Traditional Gospels* (San Francisco: HarperSanFrancisco, 1997), offers a clear and easily understood refutation of the more radical scholars' claims and points believers to reassuring solid ground for continuing belief in Jesus. See also his *Living Jesus: Learning the Heart of the Gospel* (San Francisco: HarperSanFrancisco, 1999) for this New Testament professor's positive restatement of the role of the resurrected Jesus for the life of faith. Also worthy of study is Dale C. Allison, Jr., *The Historical Christ and the Theological Jesus* (Grand Rapids MI: Eerdmans Publishing, 2009).

3. Charles H. Gabriel, "I Stand Amazed in the Presence," 1905.

Chapter 12

A Question about God

"My God, my God, why have you forsaken me?"
(Mark 15:34)

Finally I must confront, in all its mysterious horror, the unforgettable question of Jesus from the cross: "My God, my God, why have you forsaken me?" Biblical scholars call this the Cry of Dereliction, employing a word (dereliction) so seldom heard that its oddness draws us up short. As well it should. With these words, the one worshiped by Christians as the incarnate member of the Triune God goes to his death with an agonizing question about God on his lips. For any who question if Jesus really said some of the things attributed to him in the Gospels, here is one saying that is unarguably his. No one would have put such a shocking sentence in his mouth!

Some say Jesus was only quoting the opening words of Psalm 22—which he was, of course—but they contend that he then went on to quote or to recall the remainder of this psalm, which ends in confident trust and expectation. If these people are correct, Jesus moved from lament to praise, from dejection to celebration as he hung on the cross as the pioneer of our faith. Perhaps that was the case. Much within me would like to believe it happened that way. But that isn't what the Gospel writers report; they record only his devastating question. And they report it as a complete quote, not as an alluding excerpt. When I ask myself why the texts stand this way (Matthew as well as Mark report it) I find no satisfactory answer, but they do declare for all time that even in Jesus' experience, faith always has its questions—even about the presence of God.

Whenever our conversations turn to the subject of God, sitting somewhere near by is a short list of impressive words, all beginning with the prefix "omni." They are *omnipotent, omniscient,* and *omnipresent.* (For the record, these terms aren't found anywhere in the Bible; they are terms crafted to capture our culture's assumptions and some biblical statements about God.) In most minds, the "omnis" are tied to the word "God" as tightly as politics is tied to Washington, DC—you can't have one without the other(s). There are, of course, other so-called attributes of God that are predictable seatmates with this Omni Trio, but even when those other terms are absent, you can be sure the conversation begins with the assumption that God is all-powerful, all-knowing, and always present.

Given this universal starting point, it's curious that most people— even the deeply religious—want to finesse these words once the conversation gets interesting. For instance, omnipotence is dialed down to a theoretical omnipotence, say, to an all-powerful One who for the time being—but not forever!—permits much that is counter to God. Omniscience also suffers some manner of demotion so that human free will isn't exposed as a bad joke. It is agreed that God knows everything but in such a subtle, redefined way that it doesn't mean our choices are already fixed. In both these cases, it turns out that "omni" doesn't really mean a full-blown "omni." It's more of a partial, kind-of, but not-what-it-sounds-like "omni."

However, omnipresence doesn't usually suffer as many qualifications. Unlike its companions, it doesn't die through a thousand cuts—and for an obvious reason. It is one thing to hedge on God's power and to qualify God's knowledge, but it's a very different thing to hem and haw about God's presence. For if we can't claim that God is on the premises, then we must confront the possibility that we really are on our own, wandering companionless and unattended on a God-less planet. So, even as we equivocate and nuance our statements about how much God controls and how much God knows, we remain adamant that our downsized Deity is nonetheless still "with us." To lose that assurance is too great a loss, a comfort too grievous to relinquish.

Even so, I think omnipresence is as much in need of analysis and precision as its "omni" siblings. What do we mean when we say "God is with us"? Is this comparable to saying "the sky is always over us," a statement that is as true as it is ultimately unhelpful? When and how is God "with" us? Is this a one-size-fits-all claim? Are we prepared to argue that God is as present in a whorehouse as in a church house? As much "with" penthouse dwellers as "with" starving refugees in tent cities? And what might it mean that Jesus cries aloud that he is God-forsaken in the very hour Christians believe him to have been most obedient to God? Everyday honesty, if not this Cry of Dereliction, compels us to be more thoughtful in our unwavering assertion of omnipresence.

Those who pick up the Bible and read it will almost immediately encounter and then repeatedly meet the idea, if not the precise words, that "God is with us." The earth is still fresh from its creation when "the sound of the LORD God walking in the garden [of Eden]" provides the first report of God's presence "with us" (Gen 3:8). Though Adam and Eve are driven from this garden, and thus symbolically driven away from God, the ancient tales continue to present God as intimately involved in their lives and the lives of their descendants. The narrative line of the Bible then becomes highlighted by God's pledge to be "with" Israel and with those who undertake great redemptive tasks on behalf of Israel and the world: Abraham, Jacob, Moses, Joshua, David, Isaiah, Jeremiah, Jesus, Paul—to name just a few. At almost midpoint in this unfolding story we meet the beautiful, anchoring assurance that "yea, though I walk through the valley of the shadow of death, thou art with me" (Ps 23 KJV). Ultimately, the arrival of Mary's baby as "Emmanuel . . . which means 'God with us'" (Matt 1:23) clothes this grand theme in human flesh, and finally the resurrected Christ promises his disciples, and by extension his church, that he will be "with you always, to the end of the age" (Matt 28:20). Even the vision of that "end of the age" is framed in the language of "presence." John the revelator sees a vision of the descending heavenly city and hears the voice saying, "See, the home of God is among mortals. He will be with them as their God; they will be his peoples, and God himself will be with them" (Rev 21:3). Bible readers who make it all the way to this end may even remember the Hound of Heaven statement that "if I make my bed in Sheol, you [God] are there" (Ps 139:8)! The Scriptures' grand proclamation then is that our world is neither an accident nor the abandoned orphan of an Unmoved

Mover. This world and all that is within it is God's and is the object of God's concern. God is "with" it—and with us. This is the message the Bible conveys relentlessly.

At the same time, there is also a disturbingly long line of biblical voices that speaks quite frankly of the absence of God. Whoever wrote Psalm 22 stands at the head of that line, but the number of other psalmists who recorded similar moans is remarkable (e.g., Pss 13, 38, 42–43, 69, 77, 88, 142). These are a few of the many that cry out to a God who seems indifferent, withdrawn, absent. Add to their chorus the similar complaint of Job: "Oh, that I knew where I might find him. . . . If I go forward, he is not there; or backward, I cannot perceive him; on the left he hides, and I cannot behold him; I turn to the right, but I cannot see him" (23:3a, 8-9), and the declaration/complaint of Isaiah: "Truly, you are a God who hides himself" (45:15). So omnipresence, as far as the Bible's own witness is concerned, is not a term that adequately or fully describes the God of the Bible. God's presence is more nuanced, more complex within the biblical story itself.

One of the Old Testament's intriguing ways of pointing to this odd presence is to speak of God as one who "dwells in thick darkness." And surely it isn't without significance that God is troubled by David's proposal to "build me a house to live in" (2 Sam 7:5) or that Jesus never had a "home." Both of these hint of a God who will not be housed or given a fixed address like some "kept" idol.

The experience of Christians across the centuries confirms this richer and subtler biblical testimony. The monastic movement of the earliest years of Christian history candidly reports the passionate search as well as the frustration of the women and men who discovered that "ask, seek, and knock" wasn't a certain success formula for their intensely sought intimacy with God. Later voices speak of "the dark night of the soul," of seasons when divine absence rather than presence was the inexplicable reality they endured. One biographer of Martin Luther says the spiritual journey of the great sixteenth-century reformer can be summed up in his obsession with the confounding complexity of "God present and God absent, God too near and God too far, the God of wrath and the God of love, God weak and God almighty, God real and God as illusion, God hidden and God revealed."[1] Seventeenth-century mathematician, physicist, and Christian philosopher Blaise Pascal certainly stands in this lengthy queue as evidenced in his blunt summary of his own spiritual search: "A religion which does not affirm that God is hidden is not true."

Closer to our time there is the remarkable life of the World War II-era British pastor, J. B. Phillips. Aware of how little of the authorized translation of the Bible (King James Version) was being understood by young people in his parish, Phillips began to paraphrase portions of the New Testament for them; it was a project he began in the underground tunnels and bomb shelters of London during the Nazi blitzkrieg. The exceptional quality of his work soon became known outside Phillips's parish, and with the assistance of C. S. Lewis in 1960 he finally published the complete New Testament under the title *The New Testament in Modern English*. English readers around the world were fascinated and blessed by his work, making his text an international bestseller and motivating others to offer their own paraphrases or translations, Ken Taylor (*The Living Bible*) and Eugene Peterson (*The Message*) being the best known. Phillips went on to write several helpful little books about the Bible and the Christian faith, including his classic, *Your God Is Too Small*. Yet a major facet of Phillips's personal life is nowhere evident in these books, namely the fact that for decades, he suffered from unrelieved clinical depression. Though he sought help from every quarter—including the direct intervention of God—his days and nights remained shrouded in sadness. Almost all of his daily ministries, writing, and translation work were done in an emotional darkness as bleak as the bomb shelters in which he'd first begun them. He saw few happy moments of God's ever being "with" him in anything like a shining presence.[2]

A poignant ditto of Phillips's faith story may be seen in the anguish of the Roman Catholic heroine, Mother Teresa. This quiet lady garnered the entire world's admiration and even a Nobel Peace Prize for her astounding work among the most wretched cast-offs on the streets of Calcutta. But all the books and articles praising her selfless service rose to higher appreciation when, contrary to her desires,

her personal letters were posthumously published in 2007. In one
letter, actually a prayer, she wrote,

> Lord, my God, who am I that You should forsake me? The Child
> of your Love—and now become as the most hated one—the one—
> You have thrown away as unwanted—unloved. . . . Where is my
> Faith—even deep down right in there is nothing, but emptiness &
> darkness—My God—how painful is this unknown pain—I have
> no Faith. . . . So many unanswered questions live within me afraid
> to uncover them—because of the blasphemy—If there be God—
> please forgive me. . . .[3]

Surely, before offering any quick, glib assurances that "God is with
us," we must listen to and reckon with these somber counter testi-
monies coming from dismayed seekers and lovers of God. There's
simply too much evidence of God's absence to deny that it, too, is a
part of faith's experience. Jesus' Cry of Dereliction is of course the
most disturbing testimony of all.

How then do I respond to Jesus' question and the painful
questions about God's presence that it surfaces? Though I don't want
to appear maddeningly evasive, I must begin with the obvious. Jesus'
question was addressed to God, not us. All of the so-called Lament
Psalms (Psalm 22 is but one of many) are of the same nature; they are
cries not only *for* God but also and most pointedly *to* God. The proper
one to answer them, therefore, is God, not any mortal who is
presumptuous enough to think that he or she has an inside track on
the mind of the Eternal. Whatever gestures you or I make toward
some response to the Cry of Dereliction will fall short.

This being said, I risk these few words. First, Jesus' question was
why God had forsaken him, not *if* God had forsaken him. His own
words therefore declare that he was indeed forsaken by God in that
hour. Though piety rushes in to deny this and protests that God
would never have done such a thing, Jesus' own words say otherwise.
Yes, a nest of thorny and ultimately unsolvable theological issues lies
hidden in plain sight here. (For example: If God is One, how can one
person of the Godhead be "dropped" by another?) But the text says
what it says. This being so, I can only be stunned by the cataclysmic

anguish transpiring within the Godhead that is exposed to us in Jesus' words. Such was the unimaginable enormity of the event of Golgotha within God's own self.

Second, the New Testament gives us reason to believe that this absence was necessary for the full measure of sin's wickedness and its judgment to be complete. In Paul's words, Jesus "was made sin for us" (2 Cor 5:21), his identification with us and the sin so dear to us now being so complete that a holy God had to turn away.

Third, whatever may be the theological "why" of this history-upending moment—and I admit I'm now rushing away from the bafflement of it—I delight in the emotional and spiritual consequence of Jesus' forsakenness. For his "My God, my God, why?" means there is no depth of human dereliction to which Jesus is a stranger. Through his suffering he became a companion and fellow sufferer with all those who also feel abandoned by God and humanity. As F. F. Bruce writes, "When they call out of the depths to God, he who called out of the depths to God on Good Friday knows what it feels like. But there is this difference; he is with them now to strengthen them—no one was there to strengthen him."[4] He endured God's abandonment that we might never have to. This is all I know to say in response to Jesus' experience.

There is perhaps more, however, that can be said about our own experience with the presence and absence of God. For that I find guidance from biblical scholar Samuel Terrien. As Terrien studied the stories and faith utterances of the Bible, he was compelled to discard the standard "omni" attributes and to declare that the "elusiveness" of God actually matched the texts. Terrien therefore spoke and wrote of *The Elusive Presence* of God.[5] Respecting the ambiguous, both/and testimony of Scripture as well as the record of believers' experience, Terrien taught that God's presence is always an elusive presence, a presence that refuses to be pinned down to any sacred place or ritual or text. God was and is God, free and sovereign, and therefore it is beyond us to hog-tie and guarantee on cue a sighting, an encounter, or an audience with the Living One. We have no net sufficient to ensnare this God or make of this God a tethered, predictable object.

I think Terrien's truest help, however, comes with the next step he takes. Writing as an Old Testament scholar, he makes the case that the majority of the ancient Israelites did not have the kind of electrifying spiritual encounters with God that are reported of persons like Abraham, Jacob, or Moses. The Israelites heard of these events in the context of their great worship festivals when the stories of the ancestors were rehearsed dramatically for the worshipers' benefit. And from these stories Israelite worshipers drew hope that the God of their fathers would one day appear and deal with them and the world in the dazzling ways of transformation and triumph as of old. Thus, the worship of Israel was a combination of commemoration and of anticipation, a time to remember and a time to kindle hope. But for the time being, in this season of limited experiencing of God's presence, the operative challenge for Israel was faith, or trust. The Elusive One, the One known to their ancestors and the One promised to their descendants, was present with them by faith. The Living One was "with" them, but in such an elusive way that it required trust in, rather than certainty of, that presence.

Although Terrien marshals a daunting amount of scholarly support for his reconstruction of the spiritual life of the ancient Israelites, it is impossible to know if his interpretation is correct. But I'm drawn to its plausibility; it sounds right if for no other reason than that it squares with my own spiritual journey and that of so many others.

Like Terrien's Israelites of old, I find that my faith life is anchored in yesterday, in the stories of what happened long ago. My present-day moments of ecstasy and/or intimacy with God are far fewer than some might want to believe. For the most part I lift one foot up and put one foot down, trudging all the way to the New Jerusalem town—just like everyone else. Thankfully, there do come times, while I'm pondering Scripture or while I'm engaged in worship with others, when my imagination catches sight of a fairer, grander Way and Place—a nanosecond vision of God's endgame. It's only a peephole glimpse, not a panoramic mural; a cupful, not a bucket load. But it's enough to generate conviction and hope and, if I'm not a total Scrooge, even to prompt a smidgeon of love and compassion. I live, as did Israel, in the middle times, sustained by commemoration and anticipation, and strengthened to keep on pursuing this wondrous Jesus way by means of participation in thoughtful Christian worship, its rituals, its texts, its prayers, its songs, its generative power.[6]

Thus, my faith in "God with us" is sustained not by daily epiphanies or frequent theophanies but by trust that what I've been told is true and by fleeting impressions that it really is true and will be so one day in final, full measure. This faith and hope are nurtured by a community that shares the conviction that God is with us supremely in the person of Jesus and his lingering Spirit.

Where do our emotions enter into this? I would be deceiving myself and misleading you to say that my feelings do not enter into the picture at all. Indeed, if I were to draw my conclusions about God's presence from our ways of talking about it, it would appear that God's presence is unknown apart from our feelings. Tears, warmth, safety, exaltation—these are some of the feelings I hear most often mentioned as evidence of God's presence. And I cannot claim to be exempt from saying the same. For example, in worship services I've often been reassuringly moved by something that was said or done, or just by the total experience of the moment. I interpreted my positive emotional response as evidence that God's presence was indeed in that place and moment—as presumably Jesus promised it would be (Matt 18:20). But sometimes I've then been blind-sided by a very different reading of the same service coming from another who also was present. Were our opposite readings due to our cultural backgrounds or our liturgical expectations or our differing spiritual maturity? How can the same event be perceived so differently? How much confidence can we place in our feelings?

As a volunteer hospital chaplain, I once stood at the bedside of a badly injured five-year-old. I was the one who had to tell her that her father and brothers and sister had been killed in a car-train collision the night before and that her mother was in an adjoining room, unconscious, in critical condition. The only emotions I recall in those horrid moments I spent with that little girl were unbearable sadness, dread, and emptiness. But dare I conclude that God was not present in that moment, with that child and with me? Again, when I marched with a double-dozen openly gay people up the main street of my city, a lighted candle in my hand in silent vigil and remembrance of the hundreds who had died of AIDS, was my out-of-body feeling a sign of God's presence with us? Or was it simply a chemical/biological reaction to my engaging in a demonstration that was very much outside my comfort zone? And what of J. B. Phillips and Mother Teresa and the rest, who persevered in heroically doing what they knew and could do that was right and good, even if they heard not a peep from Beyond signaling any interest, let alone approval?

Have we not all had occasions when, in retrospect, we realize the divine presence was perhaps nearer than we realized, yet we brushed it off with a shrug? It wasn't packaged right or it didn't feel like we imagined a God moment should feel. I got an inkling of this one Thanksgiving holiday as I stood with a crowd at the far end of a lengthy airport hallway. We'd been told that all arriving passengers were funneled down this hallway and that we could greet our guests as they emerged from that hallway. So there we bunched, all of us straining our eyes down that well-lit hallway, studying every figure, every gait, every tilt of the head, every cap and coat of those appearing at the far end, hoping to identify our party. But after many minutes of eager, fruitless waiting, I began to wonder if perhaps my guests had arrived through a separate entrance and were already at the luggage pickup area looking for me.

That moment of second-guessing was an occasion to begin wondering how often I have been sure I knew exactly when and where and how God would appear and be with me, only to discover that perhaps God "came on an earlier flight" and was now milling about within the terminal, say, over there helping that single mom with her three kids or assisting that foreign visitor trying to read the airport's English directional signs. Could God really be "with" us—in the same space—but in a manner unacknowledged by us? The biblical character of Jacob is not the only one who qualifies to say, "Surely the LORD is in this place—and I did not know it" (Gen 28:16).

For many reasons I cannot be content therefore to specify *the* place or to name *the* feelings that are a certain indicator of God's presence. Though I can't refute the near-universal judgment that we do feel

God's presence in our viscera, I can't accept the adequacy of that single barometer. God may be present in the very places and moments when I least feel that presence. God may be present in the silence when I need to be shut up unto my own soul-sorting work. God may be present as an Enemy keeping me from a harmful practice. God may be present as a silently grieving Presence, speechlessly horrified at the devastations we have wreaked upon creation and our neighbors.

Like Terrien's believers of biblical times, we are the recipients of stories of what once was and glimpses of what someday will be. But for now we live in the uneasy middle time, trusting that the One who was and who is to come is also with us now, regardless of our awareness of that presence. This brave belief finds its renewal come Sunday, in the "meetinghouse," where the stories are retold and the grand finale is glimpsed. Therefore, wherever else this gracious, elusive One may choose to meet me, my best hope of keeping the faith that God is with *me* is by entering into the wild promise that God is with *us*.

Jesus, my imagination cannot enter that holy space where once, for me and all us sinners, you experienced the loss that was greater than life itself. You lost your God as your reward for loving your God and for loving us. Thank you. If ever I am called upon to endure a fraction of the same, help me not to cherish what I think I know more than I cherish doing what I know I should. Help me to trust you in the dark. Lead me to the light. Amen.

Notes

1. Martin Marty, *Martin Luther* (New York: Penguin Books, 2004) 10.

2. See Vera Phillips and Edwin Robertson, *J. B. Phillips: The Wounded Healer* (Grand Rapids MI: Eerdmans Publishing, n.d.) and Phillips's posthumously published autobiography, *The Price of Success*.

3. *Mother Teresa: Come Be My Light* (New York: Doubleday Books, 2007), cited by David Van Biema, "Her Agony," *Time* 170/10 (3 September 2007): 36–43.

4. F. F. Bruce, *The Hard Sayings of Jesus* (Downers Grove IL: Intervarsity Press, 1983) 250.

5. See Samuel Terrien, *The Elusive Presence: The Heart of Biblical Theology* (New York: Harper & Row, 1978) for the full development of Terrien's ideas.

6. My own attempt to delineate this kind of worship is in my *Seeking the Face of God: Evangelical Worship Reconceived* (Macon GA: Nurturing Faith, Inc., 2013).

Chapter 13

Questions, Anyone?

The Way. That was one of the first names given to the Jesus movement. Early followers of the Nazarene didn't pretend to "have already reached the goal" (Phil 3:12) or claim that their knowledge was more than "only in part" (1 Cor 13:9). They were simply pilgrims, following the Jesus way.

It would fall to later well-intending generations to transform The Way into The Loop, too often closing the open-endedness of the way and converting it into a fortress to be defended, a circle within which to fight, a noose used to choke the spirit's breath. But the way to The Way still remains open. A faithful following of Jesus, "the pioneer and perfecter of our faith" (Heb 11:2), is still possible—even with questions and openness to all that life dumps on us.

There is, of course, much more to be found in the church's history than a persistent narrowing, just as there is more to freedom than the liberty to jettison what others have deemed valuable. One would be a fool with a capital F to discard the Spirit's working in the millennia before we made our brief, poor appearance on history's stage. On my library shelves are thousands upon thousands of words of some of history's finest theologians. I still read them with respect, for I don't want to forget how we arrived where we are. But I cannot live in the world of their thinking, in the world of their wrestling with the Mystery as it presented itself to them in their day. Their answers are *their* answers. I must be faithful in this hour and offer, as best I can, *my* answers. This calls for me to listen respectfully to their answers and drink as much wisdom as my little cup will hold. But then I must exercise a God-given freedom to ask my own questions and find my own answers. Faithfulness itself asks as much from each of us: to affirm from the heart only what the Spirit allows us to see without denigrating the problematic remainder. What we must not do is pretend that *all* these answers from the past have viability or authenticity for us, within us. That's more luggage than any pilgrim can carry.

At its heart, therefore, my concern is with the *spirit* of Christian witness in this fractious world. A kinder, gentler Christianity is in order. This is so for at least two reasons. First, it is needed because thoughtful Christians do have questions and are weighing options and coming to answers—too often on their own. Many feel compelled to hide this internal sifting from fellow Christians, reluctant to tell their Sunday school class or Bible study group that, for example, "hell" and maybe even "heaven" don't make much sense to them currently. The consequence of this concealed searching is that too many professing Christians feel hollow, for within them there's a public, Sunday-morning true believer and a hidden, not-so-sure-about-all-this-stuff seeker. But the seeker is denied daylight and therefore the Amen of the believer grows fainter Sunday by Sunday. Can anyone begin to estimate the excitement, let alone the authenticity, that could flow through the Christian community if "answerizing" were outlawed and "working on our stuff" were given wholehearted encouragement?

A second reason to seek a kinder and gentler Christian witness is that our world will entertain no other kind of witness. Evangelism at gunpoint will no longer work—if it ever did. Moreover, a hundred factors make it incredibly difficult if not downright stupid to stride onto the twenty-first-century world stage and claim to have The Final Answer. No doubt we Christians could use a greater militancy, but without a huge helping of humility within that militancy, we will gain nothing and lose even more. Who can measure the impact of a return to the originating mindset of the Way wherein believers sought not to rule the world but only to follow the Lamb within the world?

I believe the first step into this more gracious Christianity is the legitimization of searching questions within Christian discipleship. This is simply honoring the ancient practice of "faith seeking understanding," even though that practice has in some quarters been discarded in favor of "knowledge being confirmed." Christians who claim the freedom to stop and to interrogate openly all things, who are "free indeed" as Jesus promised (John 8:32 KJV), are the ones who give me hope for the future of this faith.

Christian philosopher Elton Trueblood once lamented that people "hear about the answers before they have felt the problems in any real sense. This," he said, "is what makes undergraduate education so nearly impossible—the teacher has to give the answers too soon." He contended that "we do not understand the answers if we read only the answers" and that "a faith that has not been tested is not only not appreciated, it is not even understood."[1] Soil that is saturated with answers alone yields crusaders and fanatics; it seldom nurtures people in whom the fruit of the Spirit (Gal 5:22-23) is visible. When the questions of life and of faith are felt, yes *felt* (as Trueblood said) and grappled with existentially and intellectually, then deep, rich soil is available for the growth of love, joy, peace, patience, kindness, generosity, faithfulness, gentleness, and self-control.

Page after page of church history documents that the grandest faith emerges from a painfully honest search for one's own way and answers. I referred to John Wesley earlier in this book because his is an honored place in the history of Great Britain as well as in Christian theology. His pioneering eighteenth-century labors as the founder of Methodism not only reshaped the British moral landscape but also injected a restoring zeal into the Protestant church of his day. Still, Wesley had his questions. His journals and his biographers tell us that his was a tested faith. In early adulthood, his ministry, though fervent in spirit, came to utter defeat and a spiritual dead end. In later life he twice attempted to marry, but his efforts were futile. When he finally did marry, that strife-ridden disaster ended after fifteen unhappy years. He and his younger brother and colleague in the formation of Methodism, Charles, eventually became estranged and in their final years seldom saw one another.

This is hardly the vaunted stuff of "the victorious Christian life." It's the story of real life, life as we all know it—filled with questions and persevering faith. The ultimate witness to Wesley's likeness to the rest of us can be seen in a letter he wrote to Charles in the sixty-third year of his life (June 27, 1766). In it he confessed, "I do not love God.

I never did. Therefore I never believed, in the Christian sense of the word. Therefore, I am only an honest heathen . . . . And yet, to be so employed of God!"[2] This is a most stunning statement. Nobody knows just how we are to interpret these words. But for our purposes, it is enough to know that this great man of God was also unimpressed by his résumé, a man with abiding questions about himself and thus the sincerity of his faith. But this did not cause him to renounce that faith or resign his work. I would suggest that his greatness arose in no small part precisely because his faith included humbling, admitted questions as well as dogged trust.

Consider also the revelation of Mother Teresa's travails presented in the previous chapter. The lethal depths of the questions swirling within the soul of such a great Christian leave us hushed. Mother Teresa's interior life was one of turmoil and searching, a fact she had no desire to parade. In spite of her personal anguish, she remained on the Way, determined to let her outward record be one of following Jesus. That record will stand and be all the more instructive because we now know that soul-searing questions were so much a part of her story.

Even so, is it not a shame that both of these great saints felt it necessary to conceal their struggles? Wesley told only his brother, and Mother Teresa told only her diary! Not that one needs to broadcast one's soul searches on every social media outlet available—but how sad it is that emptiness and questioning are often hidden as unworthy of faith itself.

Will the content of our faith remain the same if the interrogatory mode is granted a legitimate and even an appreciated place? Probably not. But that loss is not to be feared. I quoted Elton Trueblood above; now hear him again. In a book that he characterized as "representing more than forty years of mental struggle," Trueblood said, "It is a mark of maturity to believe fewer doctrines, but to believe them with greater intensity."[3] I find this judgment true to my own experience. The older I become, the less I need to believe as many things as I once thought. Now, less is more, and though the number of my beliefs has diminished, the character of my belief has deepened. As Protestant theologian Reinhold Niebuhr once said, "There was a time when

I had all the answers. My real growth began when I discovered that the questions to which I had the answers were not the important questions."[4]

Father Walter Burghardt, a seldom-disappointing Jesuit preacher, has written of the disorienting years he faced when Pope John XXIII's Vatican II "modernizing" of the Church unfolded. The patterns of Catholic thought and worship were revolutionized, and so was the way Burghardt understood himself and his role as a minister of the gospel. He says,

In the early 60's a young lady consulted me on a religious issue. As was my wont, I gave her the answer—with consummate clarity, impersonal objectivity, undoubted certitude. She looked at me for a moment, then asked very simply: "And what do *you* think?" I gulped, visibly and audibly. I had always taken for granted that any answer I gave anyone was my answer. For the first time it struck me hammerlike, 't ain't necessarily so. I did not realize it then, but I had touched a turning point. At 50 . . . [It was] liberating, too . . . the growing realization . . . that I need not come to others with a hatful of answers, a sackful of solutions: they no longer believed I had them! I touch others most effectively when I come to them with my own brokenness. Not fearless or tearless, unscarred and unshaken. Like Christ, I am a wounded healer. . . .[5]

I sat one afternoon with a heartbroken grandmother, a woman of longtime church involvement and of sincere Christian faith. A recent series of tragedies (gruesome accidental deaths, divorces, the death of a spouse, financial reverses, illnesses) had befallen her, tragedies of such magnitude as to make all the preceding trials in her life seem trivial. Now, she was even the caretaker for a teenaged granddaughter. The woman was crushed.

Almost inaudibly, she mumbled, "I cannot pray or even think about God, let alone feel God's presence. It is horrible." After moments of agonizing silence she continued. "Worst of all," she said, pointing to the reception area outside my office, "I am being a horrible example to my precious granddaughter out there. I should be a model of faith for her, but I'm just a puddle of confusion—I can't answer my own questions, let alone hers." I let the pain of her state-ment fill the room, not daring to push against it with "answerizing." This was holy ground.

I don't recall my precise words when I finally replied, but I hope they were to the effect that her granddaughter was probably better served by her genuineness than she could imagine. A grandmother's honesty and persistence in defiant trust were the best testimony she could give to that child. Out of the depths of her darkness, she was demonstrating that faith is always something other and more than just an answer.

Only the stonehearted or the empty-headed have no questions about God and life's journey and destination. Jesus certainly had them. From his questions, we gain light to deal with our own ques-tions and receive training in listening to the questions of others. Until we are sure that Jesus is the answer—or even if we never reach that ground—his questions remain the most important ones, the ones that can lead us to life.

NOTES

1. Elton Trueblood, *Philosophy of Religion* (New York: Harper & Row, 1957) 20.

2. John Wesley to Charles Wesley, Letters of John Wesley, Wesley Center Online, <http://wesley.nnu.edu/john-wesley/the-letters-of-john-wesley/wesleys-letters-1766b/#Seven>.

3. Elton Trueblood, *A Place to Stand* (New York: Harper & Row, 1969) 7, 32.

4. Elton Trueblood, *The Common Ventures of Life* (New York: Harper & Row Chapelbooks, 1965) 95.

5. Walter Burghardt, *Seasons that Laugh or Weep: Musings on the Human Journey* (New York: Paulist Press, 1983) 75–76.

Other available titles from

#Connect
Reaching Youth Across the Digital Divide
Brian Foreman

Reaching our youth across the digital divide is a struggle for parents, ministers, and other adults who work with Generation Z—today's teenagers. *#Connect* leads readers into the technological landscape, encourages conversations with teenagers, and reminds us all to be the presence of Christ in every facet of our lives.   *978-1-57312-693-9 120 pages/pb* **$13.00**

Beginnings
A Reverend and a Rabbi Talk About the Stories of Genesis
Michael Smith and Rami Shapiro

Editor Aaron Herschel Shapiro describes storytelling as an "infinite game" because stories "must be retold—not just repeated, but reinvented, reimagined, and reexperienced" to remain vital in the world. Mike and Rami continue their conversations from the *Mount and Mountain* books, exploring the places where their traditions intersect and diverge, listening to each other as they respond to the stories of creation, of Adam and Eve, Cain and Abel, Noah, Jacob, and Joseph.   *978-1-57312-772-1 202 pages/pb* **$18.00**

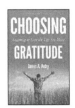

Choosing Gratitude
Learning to Love the Life You Have
James A. Autry

Autry reminds us that gratitude is a choice, a spiritual—not social—process. He suggests that if we cultivate gratitude as a way of being, we may not change the world and its ills, but we can change our response to the world. If we fill our lives with moments of gratitude, we will indeed love the life we have.   *978-1-57312-614-4 144 pages/pb* **$15.00**

Choosing Gratitude 365 Days a Year
Your Daily Guide to Grateful Living
James A. Autry and Sally J. Pederson

Filled with quotes, poems, and the inspired voices of both Pederson and Autry, in a society consumed by fears of not having "enough"—money, possessions, security, and so on—this book suggests that if we cultivate gratitude as a way of being, we may not change the world and its ills, but we can change our response to the world.   *978-1-57312-689-2 210 pages/pb* **$18.00**

To order call **1-800-747-3016** or visit **www.helwys.com**

Contextualizing the Gospel
A Homiletic Commentary on 1 Corinthians
Brian L. Harbour

Harbour examines every part of Paul's letter, providing a rich resource for those who want to struggle with the difficult texts as well as the simple texts, who want to know how God's word—all of it—intersects with their lives today. *978-1-57312-589-5 240 pages/pb* **$19.00**

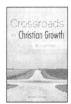

Crossroads in Christian Growth
W. Loyd Allen

Authentic Christian life presents spiritual crises and we struggle to find a hero walking with God at a crossroads. With wisdom and sincerity, W. Loyd Allen presents Jesus as our example and these crises as stages in the journey of growth we each take toward maturity in Christ. *978-1-57312-753-0 164 pages/pb* **$15.00**

A Divine Duet
Ministry and Motherhood
Alicia Davis Porterfield, ed.

Each essay in this inspiring collection is as different as the mother-minister who wrote it, from theologians to chaplains, inner-city ministers to rural-poverty ministers, youth pastors to preachers, mothers who have adopted, birthed, and done both. *978-1-57312-676-2 146 pages/pb* **$16.00**

Ethics as if Jesus Mattered
Essays in Honor of Glen H. Stassen
Rick Axtell, Michelle Tooley, Michael L. Westmoreland-White, eds.

Ethics as if Jesus Mattered will introduce Stassen's work to a new generation, advance dialogue and debate in Christian ethics, and inspire more faithful discipleship just as it honors one whom the contributors consider a mentor. *978-1-57312-695-3 234 pages/pb* **$18.00**

Ezekiel (Smyth & Helwys Annual Bible Study series)
God's Presence in Performance
William D. Shiell

Through a four-session Bible study for individuals and groups, Shiell interprets the book of Ezekiel as a four-act drama to be told to adult, children, and youth groups living out their faith in a strange, new place. The book encourages congregations to listen to God's call, accept where God has planted them, surrender the shame of their past, receive a new heart from God, and allow God to breathe new life into them.

Teaching Guide 978-1-57312-755-4 192 pages/pb **$14.00**

Study Guide 978-1-57312-756-1 126 pages/pb **$6.00**

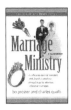

Marriage Ministry: A Guidebook

Bo Prosser and Charles Qualls

This book is equally helpful for ministers, for nearly/newlywed couples, and for thousands of couples across our land looking for fresh air in their marriages.   *1-57312-432-X 160 pages/pb* **$16.00**

A Hungry Soul Desperate to Taste God's Grace

Honest Prayers for Life

Charles Qualls

Part of how we *see* God is determined by how we *listen* to God. There is so much noise and movement in the world that competes with images of God. This noise would drown out God's beckoning voice and distract us. Charles Qualls's newest book offers readers prayers for that journey toward the meaning and mystery of God.   *978-1-57312-648-9 152 pages/pb* **$14.00**

If Jesus Isn't the Answer . . . He Sure Asks the Right Questions!

J. Daniel Day

Taking eleven of Jesus' questions as its core, Day invites readers into their own conversation with Jesus. Equal parts testimony, theological instruction, pastoral counseling, and autobiography, the book is ultimately an invitation to honest Christian discipleship.

978-1-57312-797-4 148 pages/pb **$16.00**

I'm Trying to Lead . . . Is Anybody Following?

The Challenge of Congregational Leadership in the Postmodern World

Charles B. Bugg

Bugg provides us with a view of leadership that has theological integrity, honors the diversity of church members, and reinforces the brave hearts of church leaders who offer vision and take risks in the service of Christ and the church.   *978-1-57312-731-8 136 pages/pb* **$13.00**

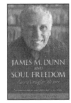

James M. Dunn and Soul Freedom

Aaron Douglas Weaver

James Milton Dunn, over the last fifty years, has been the most aggressive Baptist proponent for religious liberty in the United States. Soul freedom—voluntary, uncoerced faith and an unfettered individual conscience before God—is the basis of his understanding of church-state separation and the historic Baptist basis of religious liberty.   *978-1-57312-590-1 224 pages/pb* **$18.00**

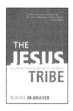

The Jesus Tribe
Following Christ in the Land of the Empire
Ronnie McBrayer

The Jesus Tribe fleshes out the implications, possibilities, contradictions, and complexities of what it means to live within the Jesus Tribe and in the shadow of the American Empire.

978-1-57312-592-5 208 pages/pb **$17.00**

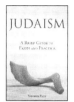

Judaism
A Brief Guide to Faith and Practice
Sharon Pace

Sharon Pace's newest book is a sensitive and comprehensive introduction to Judaism. What is it like to be born into the Jewish community? How does belief in the One God and a universal morality shape the way in which Jews see the world? How does one find meaning in life and the courage to endure suffering? How does one mark joy and forge community ties?

978-1-57312-644-1 144 pages/pb **$16.00**

Living Call
An Old Church and a Young Minister Find Life Together
Tony Lankford

This light look at church and ministry highlights the dire need for fidelity to the vocation of church leadership. It also illustrates Lankford's conviction that the historic, local congregation has a beautiful, vibrant, and hopeful future.

978-1-57312-702-8 112 pages/pb **$12.00**

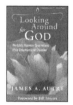

Looking Around for God
The Strangely Reverent Observations of an Unconventional Christian
James A. Autry

Looking Around for God, Autry's tenth book, is in many ways his most personal. In it he considers his unique life of faith and belief in God. Autry is a former Fortune 500 executive, author, poet, and consultant whose work has had a significant influence on leadership thinking.

978-157312-484-3 144 pages/pb **$16.00**

Meeting Jesus Today
For the Cautious, the Curious, and the Committed
Jeanie Miley

Meeting Jesus Today, ideal for both individual study and small groups, is intended to be used as a workbook. It is designed to move readers from studying the Scriptures and ideas within the chapters to recording their journey with the Living Christ.

978-1-57312-677-9 320 pages/pb **$19.00**

The Ministry Life
101 Tips for Ministers' Spouses
John and Anne Killinger

While no pastor does his or her work alone, roles for a spouse or partner are much more flexible and fluid in the twenty-first century than they once were. Spouses who want to support their minister-mates' vocation may wonder where to begin. The Killingers' suggestions are notable for their range of interests; whatever your talents may be, the Killingers have identified a way to put those gifts to work in tasks both large and small.

978-1-57312-769-1 252 pages/pb **$19.00**

The Ministry Life
101 Tips for New Ministers
John Killinger

Sharing years of wisdom from more than fifty years in ministry and teaching, *The Ministry Life: 101 Tips for New Ministers* by John Killinger is filled with practical advice and wisdom for a minister's day-to-day tasks as well as advice on intellectual and spiritual habits to keep ministers of any age healthy and fulfilled.

978-1-57312-662-5 244 pages/pb **$19.00**

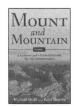

Mount and Mountain
Vol. 1: A Reverend and a Rabbi Talk About the Ten Commandments
Rami Shapiro and Michael Smith

Mount and Mountain represents the first half of an interfaith dialogue—a dialogue that neither preaches nor placates but challenges its participants to work both singly and together in the task of reinterpreting sacred texts. Mike and Rami discuss the nature of divinity, the power of faith, the beauty of myth and story, the necessity of doubt, the achievements, failings, and future of religion, and, above all, the struggle to live ethically and in harmony with the way of God.

978-1-57312-612-0 144 pages/pb **$15.00**

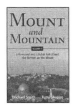

Mount and Mountain
Vol. 2: A Reverend and a Rabbi Talk About the Sermon on the Mount
Rami Shapiro and Michael Smith

This book, focused on the Sermon on the Mount, represents the second half of Mike and Rami's dialogue. In it, Mike and Rami explore the text of Jesus' sermon cooperatively, contributing perspectives drawn from their lives and religious traditions and seeking moments of illumination.

978-1-57312-654-0 254 pages/pb **$19.00**

Of Mice and Ministers
Musings and Conversations About Life, Death, Grace, and Everything

Bert Montgomery

With stories about pains, joys, and everyday life, *Of Mice and Ministers* finds Jesus in some unlikely places and challenges us to do the same. From tattooed women ministers to saying the "N"-word to the brotherly kiss, Bert Montgomery takes seriously the lesson from Psalm 139—where can one go that God is not already there? *978-1-57312-733-2 154 pages/pb* **$14.00**

Overcoming Adolescence
Growing Beyond Childhood into Maturity

Marion D. Aldridge

In *Overcoming Adolescence*, Marion D. Aldridge poses questions for adults of all ages to consider. His challenge to readers is one he has personally worked to confront: to grow up *all the way*—mentally, physically, academically, socially, emotionally, and spiritually. The key involves not only knowing how to work through the process but also how to recognize what may be contributing to our perpetual adolescence.

978-1-57312-577-2 156 pages/pb **$17.00**

Preacher Breath
Sermon & Essays

Kyndall Rae Rothaus

"The task of preaching is such an oddly wonderful, strangely beautiful experience. . . . Kyndall Rothaus's *Preacher Breath* is a worthy guide, leading the reader room by room with wisdom, depth, and a spiritual maturity far beyond her years, so that the preaching house becomes a holy, joyful home. . . . This book is soul kindle for a preacher's heart."
—Danielle Shroyer
Pastor and Author of *The Boundary-Breaking God*
978-1-57312-734-9 208 pages/pb **$16.00**

Quiet Faith
An Introvert's Guide to Spiritual Survival

Judson Edwards

In eight finely crafted chapters, Edwards looks at key issues like evangelism, interpreting the Bible, dealing with doubt, and surviving the church from the perspective of a confirmed, but sometimes reluctant, introvert. In the process, he offers some provocative insights that introverts will find helpful and reassuring. *978-1-57312-681-6 144 pages/pb* **$15.00**

Reading Deuteronomy
(Reading the Old Testament series)
A Literary and Theological Commentary
Stephen L. Cook

A lost treasure for large segments of the modern world, the book of Deuteronomy powerfully repays contemporary readers' attention. God's presence and Word in Deuteronomy stir deep longing for God and move readers to a place of intimacy with divine otherness, holism, and will for person-centered community. The consistently theological interpretation reveals the centrality of Deuteronomy for faith and counters critical accusations about violence, intolerance, and polytheism in the book. *978-1-57312-757-8 286 pages/pb* **$22.00**

Reading Hosea–Micah
(Reading the Old Testament series)
A Literary and Theological Commentary
Terence E. Fretheim

Terence E. Fretheim explores themes of indictment, judgment, and salvation in Hosea–Micah. The indictment against the people of God especially involves issues of idolatry, as well as abuse of the poor and needy. The effects of such behaviors are often horrendous in their severity. While God is often the subject of such judgments, the consequences, like fruit, grow out of the deed itself. *978-1-57312-687-8 224 pages/pb* **$22.00**

Reflective Faith
A Theological Toolbox for Women
Tony W. Cartledge

In *Reflective Faith*, Susan Shaw offers a set of tools to explore difficult issues of biblical interpretation, theology, church history, and ethics—especially as they relate to women. Reflective faith invites intellectual struggle and embraces the unknown; it is a way of discipleship, a way to love God with your mind, as well as your heart, your soul, and your strength.
978-1-57312-719-6 292 pages/pb **$24.00**
Workbook 978-1-57312-754-7 164 pages/pb **$12.00**

Sessions with Psalms (Session Bible Studies series)
Prayers for All Seasons
Eric and Alicia D. Porterfield

Sessions with Psalms is a ten-session study unit designed to explore what it looks like for the words of the psalms to become the words of our prayers. Each session is followed by a thought-provoking page of questions that allow for a deeper experience of the scriptural passages. These resource pages can be used by seminar leaders during preparation and group discussion, as well as in individual Bible study. *978-1-57312-768-4 136 pages/pb* **$14.00**

Sessions with Revelation (Session Bible Studies series)
The Final Days of Evil
David Sapp

David Sapp's careful guide through Revelation demonstrates that it is a letter of hope for believers; it is less about the last days of history than it is about the last days of evil. Without eliminating its mystery, Sapp unlocks Revelation's central truths so that its relevance becomes clear. *978-1-57312-706-6 166 pages/pb* **$14.00**

Spacious
Exploring Faith and Place
Holly Sprink

Exploring where we are and why that matters to God is an ongoing process. If we are present and attentive, God creatively and continuously widens our view of the world. *978-1-57312-649-6 156 pages/pb* **$16.00**

The Teaching Church
Congregation as Mentor
Christopher M. Hamlin / Sarah Jackson Shelton

Collected in *The Teaching Church: Congregation as Mentor* are the stories of the pastors who shared how congregations have shaped, nurtured, and, sometimes, broken their resolve to be faithful servants of God. *978-1-57312-682-3 112 pages/pb* **$13.00**

Time for Supper
Invitations to Christ's Table
Brett Younger

Some scholars suggest that every meal in literature is a communion scene. Could every meal in the Bible be a communion text? Could every passage be an invitation to God's grace? At the Lord's Table we experience sorrow, hope, friendship, and forgiveness. These meditations on the Lord's Supper help us listen to the myriad of ways God invites us to gratefully, reverently, and joyfully share the cup of Christ. *978-1-57312-720-2 246 pages/pb* **$18.00**

A Time to Laugh
Humor in the Bible

Mark E. Biddle

An extension of his well-loved seminary course on humor in the Bible, *A Time to Laugh* draws on Mark E. Biddle's command of Hebrew language and cultural subtleties to explore the ways humor was intentionally incorporated into Scripture. With characteristic liveliness, Biddle guides the reader through the stories of six biblical characters who did rather unexpected things. 978-1-57312-683-0 *164 pages/pb* **$14.00**

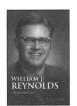

The World Is Waiting for You
Celebrating the 50th Ordination Anniversary of Addie Davis

Pamela R. Durso & LeAnn Gunter Johns, eds.

Hope for the church and the world is alive and well in the words of these gifted women. Keen insight, delightful observations, profound courage, and a gift for communicating the good news are woven throughout these sermons. The Spirit so evident in Addie's calling clearly continues in her legacy. 978-1-57312-732-5 *224 pages/pb* **$18.00**

William J. Reynolds
Church Musician

David W. Music

William J. Reynolds is renowned among Baptist musicians, music ministers, song leaders, and hymnody students. In eminently readable style, David W. Music's comprehensive biography describes Reynolds's family and educational background, his career as a minister of music, denominational leader, and seminary professor. 978-1-57312-690-8 *358 pages/pb* **$23.00**

With Us in the Wilderness
Finding God's Story in Our Lives

Laura A. Barclay

What stories compose your spiritual biography? In *With Us in the Wilderness*, Laura Barclay shares her own stories of the intersection of the divine and the everyday, guiding readers toward identifying and embracing God's presence in their own narratives.

978-1-57312-721-9 *120 pages/pb* **$13.00**

Clarence Jordan's

COTTON PATCH
Gospel

The
Complete
Collection

Hardback • 448 pages
Retail ~~50.00~~ • Your Price 25.00

Paperback • 448 pages
Retail ~~40.00~~ • Your Price 20.00

The Cotton Patch Gospel, by Koinonia Farm founder Clarence Jordan, recasts the stories of Jesus and the letters of the New Testament into the language and culture of the mid-twentieth-century South. Born out of the civil rights struggle, these now-classic translations of much of the New Testament bring the far-away places of Scripture closer to home: Gainesville, Selma, Birmingham, Atlanta, Washington D.C.

More than a translation, *The Cotton Patch Gospel* continues to make clear the startling relevance of Scripture for today. Now for the first time collected in a single, hardcover volume, this edition comes complete with a new Introduction by President Jimmy Carter, a Foreword by Will D. Campbell, and an Afterword by Tony Campolo. Smyth & Helwys Publishing is proud to help reintroduce these seminal works of Clarence Jordan to a new generation of believers, in an edition that can be passed down to generations still to come.

To order call **1-800-747-3016**
or visit **www.helwys.com**

Made in the USA
Columbia, SC
05 February 2022

55504170R00083